LINGERING GRIEF

LISTENING FOR GOD IN THE PAIN

Smyth & Helwys Publishing, Inc.
6316 Peake Road
Macon, Georgia 31210-3960
1-800-747-3016
©2007 by Smyth & Helwys Publishing
All rights reserved.
Printed in the United States of America.

The paper used in this publication meets the minimum requirements of
American National Standard for Information Sciences—
Permanence of Paper for Printed Library Materials.
ANSI Z39.48–1984. (alk. paper)

Library of Congress Cataloging-in-Publication Data

Bugg, Charles B.
Lingering grief : listening for God in the pain / Charles B. Bugg.
p. cm.
ISBN 978-1-57312-489-8 (pbk. : alk. paper)
1. Suffering—Religious aspects—Christianity. 2. Consolation.
3. Grief—Religious aspects—Christianity. I. Title.

BV4909.B84 2007
248.8'6—dc22

2007010487

LINGERING GRIEF

Listening for God in the Pain

Charles Bugg

Contents

Introduction

In 1993, Smyth & Helwys Publishing was gracious enough to publish a book I wrote, *Learning to Dream Again*. I tried to tell something of the story of our son David. In February 1983, David was diagnosed with a malignant brain tumor. That diagnosis sent not only David, but also our whole family, down a road we would never have chosen to travel.

It was a road filled with the smells of hospitals and the sounds of medical terms that frightened me with their complexity. We saw our son endure the pain of tests, surgeries, and radiation treatments. As a minister, I struggled with the issue of what seemed to me to be inexplicable suffering.

The good news is that David is very much alive. As I write this, I hear the sound of the television in our family room and know that my son is watching. While David will never have what we term a "normal life," he reminds our family of important qualities like courage, sensitivity to others, and a quiet, authentic faith in God.

Fourteen years have passed since I wrote *Learning to Dream Again*. I wanted to write about David once more. Why do I write again about David? I suppose it's because he's never far from my mind. Or maybe it's because David reminds me that life is both precious and fragile. Or maybe I need the catharsis that comes when we try to put on paper moments in the movement of life that are really too deep for words.

However, this time I want to write about more than just our family's experience. As I have traveled to different places to preach and to speak, I have found that my telling of David's story has evoked moving responses from people. Some people have promised to pray for David and my family. I haven't tracked all of these people to see if they have kept their promises, but even the expressions of care have meant so much.

The responses, though, that have profoundly moved me are the stories that people have shared with me because David's story is much like theirs. For certain, the details of the stories are different. Yet, there is a striking similarity. A young engineer tells me about an older brother who is a paraplegic. One day the older brother, while playing with his children, dived headfirst into a pile of leaves. What he didn't see was a rock buried in the leaves. His head hit the rock, and now a once physically vibrant young man is irreparably changed.

A couple gives birth to a child. They want what every mother and father desire: "As long as the child is healthy . . . ." But she's not. "Down's Syndrome," the physician says, and now the parents and their child face a multiplicity of unexpected demands. A husband notices that his wife is beginning to forget some things. Maybe it's just a "senior moment." One day, however, he gets a call from the manager of the grocery store that his wife seems confused and can't remember where she parked the car. The physician examines her and writes the word "dementia" on her chart. Just one word, but we know what it means. After a while, she no longer recognizes her husband, her children, or her grandchildren. How painful to watch intimacy become such distance.

These are just a few of the responses that my sharing of David's story have sparked in the lives of others. The common thread is grief. Nobody has physically died, but when we think about it, so much has died. Dreams we had died. Relationships changed. Whole families suddenly shifted in a psychological earthquake.

The grief continues. Certainly, time and perspective bring healing, but we see a person whom we deeply love and wonder what may have been. We don't have a funeral that at least brings some finality or gives us a point in time from which we can begin to reconstruct our lives. A child who is autistic stands in front of us. While we go on with life, the fact is that our lives and our child's life are different. If it's a husband who suffers from "Alzheimer's Disease," his wife sees the shell of what used to be. She can't help remembering the time he touched her hand, held her close, or told her, "I love you more than life itself."

I've chosen to call this experience "lingering grief." It's grief that lives with us every day and every night. It can be overwhelming. This kind of grief can make us jaded and cynical. Or it can deepen us and make us treasure life even more and fear death even less. However we respond, the grief makes a big difference in what we may have expected our lives to be, and in one way or another, we adjust to what will not adjust to us.

If you are reading this and have experienced the death of a "beloved," I hope you understand that I'm not saying the type of grief I've known with David is more severe than yours. I have been a minister long enough that in some sense, grief lingers for all of us who have experienced losses. A woman told me about her husband who had died. "Each night," she said, "I reach across the bed expecting to touch his hand. All I feel is emptiness." In the local newspaper, a child's picture is at the bottom of the obituary page. The child died two years ago, but his family pledges to remember the day of his birthday. The loss of something or someone evokes many of the same feelings regardless of whether it's a physical death, a death of a relationship, or having to let expectations that we had for someone or for ourselves die while a new reality is born.

Grief is grief, but one of my concerns is that caregiving for those who are experiencing lingering grief is often more difficult than for those who have experienced a death. For example, I have met people who have been through the experience of divorce. They remember when they stood as a couple in front of a minister and pledged, ". . . till death do us part." They parted, but it wasn't at death. It was another man, another woman, or an instance in which somebody became bored with his or her partner. For at least one person in that relationship, it wasn't death, but it sure felt that way.

"I am going through a divorce," she said. "I need to find a new church." I listened as she shared. "It's not that the people in my former church don't care for me. Many of them have called, and some have invited me for dinner," the woman continued. "But the longer this goes on, I don't think even my friends know what to do with me, and frankly I don't really know what to do with myself." She spoke about needing God but feeling distant from God and the church. "I feel angry, desperate, ashamed. My self-esteem is so low. I feel rejected, unloved. I don't even know what I want people to do for me. Most of all I know I can't put my marriage back together."

Not every story of lingering grief is the same, but she captured much of what I experienced. I felt out of control. Things were happening to David that I didn't understand. The only prognosis the neurosurgeon could give our family was "Take one day at a time." I felt isolated. I was too tired to interact with people. I was tired of explaining to people what I didn't understand myself. Each time somebody asked, "How's David doing?" I wanted to scream.

When people asked me what they could do for my family and me, all I could say was "pray." Even that sounded empty because I was having trouble praying myself. As well intentioned as some people were, I didn't know what to tell them to do. When people said, "Let me know what we can do," I was frustrated. I was trying to put one foot in front of another, and these people were asking for directions and instructions. What meant the most to my family and me were the notes, the small gifts, and the cards through which people let us know they cared.

Most painful for me was my struggle to find anything of God in David's illness. Embedded in me was the notion that you and I get what we deserve. While at some level in my mind I knew that bad things happen to good people and good things happen to bad people, I operated with a strong sense of justice. As a minister, I tried to explain the inexplicable. Without symmetry, how could we ever make any sense of anything? The doctrine of creation meant that chaos had been tamed, and we could find the hand of God at work if we simply thought long and hard enough about it.

David's diagnosis confronted me with the utter irrationality of much of life. My son had done nothing to deserve what happened to him. If God were trying to communicate some message to me, then it seemed that God had picked on the wrong person. If I needed to understand something, then why hadn't God let me be the one to have the tumor?

Like the woman going through her divorce, I felt distant from God. My vocation was to preach in the church and to the community of faith. My home Baptist church had commended me to the ministry and blessed me with ordination before I left for seminary. Wasn't seminary the place where I was supposed to learn about God and to try to give some sense to the work of God in people's lives? I remembered my course in theology. The seminary catalogue labeled it "Systematic Theology."

Perhaps I expected too much, but the word "systematic" implied order, or at least a theological frame in which the disparate pieces of life could be placed, labeled, and interpreted. Since the currency of my ministry was primarily words, I expected that I would be able to put a frame around the painful parts of people's lives to let them know God was good even when life was bad.

I was at a loss for words to explain my own journey, much less those of others. Our family was living a reality that I didn't understand. I had questions of God, for God, and about God for which I had no answers either for myself or for David or for anybody else.

I still have questions. However, while watching David each day has brought sadness, it has also reminded me of the courage it takes to accept life as it is and to continue to live with both our certainties and our uncertainties. For me, David is a model of courage. Courage is not merely taking action. Often, it is taking life as it comes, accepting what we cannot change, and not giving up on ourselves and not giving up on God.

So I write this book to myself and for myself. But I also write it for those who have told me stories of their own lingering grief. I write because I have seen courage, and I believe I have seen the goodness of God in the faces of folks who refuse to surrender even when the suffering seems overwhelming.

When I was a little boy, my parents would read me grand stories that always ended, "And they lived happily ever after." I dreamed about castles in the sky. I wanted to live someday in the place where good news was the only news. I'm much older now. Both my parents are dead. I haven't found the land of "happily ever after," but I have found people who made wherever I have been a much richer and caring place.

One of those people is Selvia Brown, administrative assistant at the M. Christopher White School of Divinity at Gardner-Webb University. When I came to be dean and to teach at the divinity school, I told Selvia that I was "technologically challenged." Selvia has taken words that I've written on legal pads and put them into a form that fits the demands of the publisher. I'm grateful for her friendship and for her gracious spirit in providing me the help I needed.

I want to dedicate this book to Mary Jean Poston and to Nelson Poston. Nelson died a few years ago, and for that reason, I wish I had written these words earlier. They are my wife's parents, my in-laws. When David was diagnosed, I thought often about my immediate family. I confess I thought little about the devastating impact that this news had on Diane's parents or my parents. All of them must have suffered enormously. Yet, what I remember is the gifts of presence and prayers that the Postons gave to our family. They grieved, but they never stopped giving of themselves. I call that love! I call that courage! It's long overdue, but I want to thank them for what they have meant to me.

Chapter One

Grief as a Common Experience

Our Common Griefs

Grief is a response to loss. Loss comes in different ways. Sometimes it is part of the natural progression of life. A child packs his bags and gets ready to head to college. His family expected that to happen. Yet, when the day comes to say good-bye, Mom and Dad cry and sniffle as they drive back home. They go to his bedroom where they used to complain about the loud music, and the silence is deafening.

Why the sadness? Something has changed, and the times that they carted their son to soccer practice and piano recitals are memories stored in pictures. That's a loss. His parents knew the day would come when their son went to college, but it doesn't make the pain any less.

In January 2003, Diane and I had our first grandchild. His name is Finn. Our daughter and son-in-law are now referred to as "Finn's parents." Unfortunately, Finn and his parents live in the Boston, Massachusetts, area. We probably see Finn and his parents about every other month. This means lots of changes in Finn between visits.

Finn and his parents came to stay with us for a week during the Christmas holidays. My grandson and I are the two early risers in our family. I take him downstairs where I can hold him on my lap, cuddle him, and read him some of his books.

That's what I expected at Christmas. After about five minutes of cuddling, Finn wiggled, stretched, pushed, shoved, and let me know that he wanted to explore the family room, kitchen, and any other place to which he could crawl. He pulled himself up and edged along tables searching for anything in reach. Instead of a cuddly baby in my arms, I had a jailbreak on my hands. Do you want to know something? I know Finn wouldn't want his granddad to hold him forever, but I miss those times when the two of us could sit, and I would look into the face of all the joy and wonder of this special gift. My primary task, now, is to move things to higher shelves and make sure Finn stays in sight.

This was expected, but it's change, and I miss the baby who's becoming a boy who one day will be a young man, and you know the way it goes. By its very nature, life is change, and if we have the courage, we will change too. In fact, if we don't adjust to the changing seasons of life, we start to look and act strange.

We hit middle age, and if we haven't noticed it before, we recognize we are getting older. We try to eat the right foods; we exercise—all of this is positive. We can stave off some of the effects of aging, but the fact is, "Toto," we are not in Kansas, and we're not twenty anymore. The good news is Dorothy and the dog returned home, but if our idyllic age is twenty, we are not going back to that home. As we age, we lose some things, and we gain some things. We grieve a full head of hair, boundless energy, and the dream we had to change the world. At the same time, hopefully we gain some wisdom, some perspective, and a more realistic view of what we have to accept and what we can help to change.

Getting older involves some grief. We realize that we are not going to be in this world forever, we start receiving the AARP magazine, and cashiers at restaurants give us the senior citizen's discount even if we don't ask for it.

How do we deal with these transitions in life? I had a friend who was going through what we sometimes call the mid-life crisis. My friend was in his late forties. He came to see me at my office. His shirt was unbuttoned almost to his stomach. Around his neck was an assortment of gold chains. His thinning hair looked as if it had fallen into a vat of "Dippety-Doo gel." "You look different," I said. That was the understatement of the year. He looked weird. Frankly, a lot of my friends still looked late forties. Evidently, someone more courageous than I called his hand. I saw him again in a few months. The chains were gone, the hair didn't look as if he had stuck his finger in an electrical socket, and thank God he had his shirt buttoned.

If we live life for any length of time, we know that there are seasons to our lives. Each season brings its gladness; each season brings its sadness. The best thing is to live into whatever we are and wherever we are in the cycle of life. Several years ago I turned sixty. My wife reminded me that Lauren Hutton, the model, said that sixty is like thirty used to be. "Since when is Lauren Hutton an expert on the aging process?" I asked. "I've seen Lauren Hutton since she turned sixty, and I remember her when she was thirty. She's still attractive," I told Diane, "but I wouldn't mistake her for thirty."

"It's on the inside," Diane said. "It's how you feel about yourself." I had just been to the orthopedist, which is now the medical specialty I support most. I had pain in my shoulder. After the X-rays, my orthopedist, who reminds me of a former National Football League linebacker and has the bedside manner to match, told me that I had tendonitis, bursitis, and arthritis in the one shoulder. I didn't know you could have all three at one time. "What should I do?" I asked. "Stop using the shoulder machine at the fitness center."

Do you realize how many machines I've had to stop using in the last few years? Since my orthopedic doctor is a person of few words, I didn't tell him about Lauren Hutton's comment that even though my birth certificate says sixty, I'm really thirty. "It's on the inside," Diane reminded me. "It's how you think and feel about yourself." In so many ways, of course, she is right. I don't want to spend my last years playing shuffleboard, living in Florida, wearing dark stretch socks, shirts with flamingoes on them, Bermuda shorts in pastel colors, and sitting around with people whose conversations center on the ailments that beset them. I take part of that back. I wouldn't mind living in Florida.

My point is that life itself is an experience in grief. To say hello to the next chapter, we have to say good-bye to the previous one. As a minister, I have been struck by the image of "journey" so prevalent in the Bible. The people of Israel were on the move. Sometimes the places they went were not places they chose. Often, the people wondered if God were able to go with them. Isn't that intriguing? Can God be with us in Babylon? Does God cross borders and accompany us to territory that is alien and hostile?

In a profound sense, that is still our question. Does God go with us through the seasons of our lives? A fourteen-year-old girl looks in the mirror and sees "zits" and a body that looks misshapen and, in her words, "weird." She feels strange. No longer a girl, but she's still not the woman she will become. The rules her parents set make her feel that she is a slave to people who don't really understand her and are out to ruin her life. Her self-esteem slithers along the floor because she doesn't understand herself, and nobody else understands her.

She remembers when she was baptized. Eight years old. Her parents loved her, the church loved her, and she really felt the love of God. It's amazing what six years can do. Now at fourteen she struggles to feel any intimacy with God, much less with anybody else. Shall we tell her that she's going through a phase? Let's not. I always hated it when somebody told me that I was going through a phase. It never made me feel any better.

Maybe we should tell her that life is a sometimes arduous and difficult journey. The people of Israel certainly found that to be true. "Who are we?" they lamented. "Where is God?" they cried. Sometimes their prophets called the so-called chosen ones, "suffering servants."

Certainly, Jesus invited his followers to an uneven and often dangerous journey. Jesus kept calling his followers to leave things. The disciples left fishing nets, old haunting grounds, a father and probably some mothers, and perhaps even a wife or two or three. Why don't we ever speak about the grief of these disciples? To say yes to Jesus meant that they had to say no to some very important things.

I'm not saying that you and I need to prove our love for Jesus by leaving our spouses. However, I am saying that the Bible we use is filled with stories of losing, leaving, and letting go. Those are grief experiences. God causes or at least allows grief. It's as if God blesses some grief and says that to live is to lose, to leave, and to learn to let go.

If life can be imagined as a journey, then grief is part of the trip. We expect changes. We anticipate transitions. We understand that our lives, like the world around us, have seasons. We are also affected by the grief that happens around us. Wars, oppression, poverty, environmental destruction—I know we can't take all of these issues personally; if we did, we couldn't function. But it's hard for us not to be affected by the horrible scenes of September 11, 2001, and the reminder of what political, ethnic, and religious differences can make us do to one another.

Our president said the invasion of Iraq was necessary. So many people have lost their lives or have lost parts of themselves that will change their futures. We have all lost something of our innocence, and we wonder if an eye for an eye only means that more people will lose their eyes. We go on wondering if Michael Jackson is just crazy or if he's both crazy and a child molester. We watch Britney Spears—has she lost her way or did she have any kind of moral compass in the first place? Some of us grieve the apparent values of our American society. A first grade teacher is paid as if her job is important but not that important. On the other hand, a football player who speaks as if he slept through any English grammar course he ever had is given millions of dollars because fans like the way he catches a football.

These things should cause us to grieve. What are our values? What are our priorities? The rich get richer, and the poorest around us are poorer than ever. Surely we can do better. But we don't. Does that make you or me grieve? These things linger. Sometimes houses of worship say nothing about the injustices, the filthy rich, our aging parents struggling to buy food and medicine, or children with bloated bellies and flies landing on their faces. Ethnic, political, and religious hatred gave rise to the tragedy of 9/11. Those same issues contribute to the indifference that we have toward those who are not like us.

Where is the word from the churches, the synagogues, or the mosques? Where is the word of reconciliation? As a teenager, I remember my pastor's speaking eloquently about how God had chosen the stage of human history to play out God's drama of redemption. While the message of Jesus was for all times and all places, God's embodiment had spoken to that time and place. That was a genius of our faith. God took time and place seriously. I wonder how seriously I take my time and place. Jesus was moved by the needs of people he met. He took so-called losers and told them that God loved them. Jesus had the audacity to tell a rich ruler to sell all the man had and give the proceeds to the poor. According to Jesus, that was the path to meaningful, eternal life. The ruler refused. To lose what has been the center of life, even if it's not altogether satisfying, is a grief experience.

The Varieties of Grief

Grief comes in a variety of ways—the expected transitions, the calls to change what we are accustomed to and what has been important to us, and to try to make some sense of the world in which we live. We wonder why some have more than enough and others have hardly anything, and why so much pain is inflicted on others often in the name of our deities.

Another kind of grief many have to face, however, is not expected and is painfully personal. When I was a student in the ninth grade, I was asked to do a career notebook. Each of us in the class had to pick what we wanted to be when we grew up. If I remember correctly, I wanted to be an attorney. So I researched what an attorney did, interviewed some attorneys, and wrote my career notebook. Actually, I think I wanted to be like Perry Mason in some courtroom winning every case, exonerating his client, and getting somebody else to confess to the crime. That seemed so exciting.

I was crushed when I interviewed some attorneys, and they were drowning in paperwork. "What about Perry Mason?" I asked. They laughed and assured me that being an attorney meant your staff and you had to do a lot of dull and tedious work.

Through the years I've reflected on my "career notebook." For one thing, I didn't become an attorney. But I always thought of my "career" as involving so many parts of my life other than what I did for a living. As much as I could project my life as a ninth grader, I saw myself having a spouse and family, working at some vocation, trying to contribute meaning to other's lives, and having a house I would leave in the morning and return to in time for a happy supper with my family. On the weekends, I would mow the lawn, go to a movie with my family, attend Sunday school and church, eat a nice lunch, and take a nap.

At that point in my life, everything I dreamed seemed ordered, sequential, and symmetrical. My expectations were exactly what that word implied. I expected certain events to take place. Any thought of disorder never crossed my mind. Partly, I'm sure, because when you are fifteen years old, you don't factor nightmares into your dreams. It was also because this is the way I seemed to be put together as a person. Maybe I was potty trained too soon, but I'm wired for order and balance. Later when I learned the phrase, "Plan your work and work your plan," those words became my mantra. Flexibility has never been my strong suit.

I remember summer vacations when my children were smaller. It was hard for me to take a vacation. Vacation meant "downtime." Not every moment was planned. When we visited Diane's parents in Kentucky, we would spend several hours a day sitting on the back porch making "small talk." Actually, it wasn't small talk. The family was catching up and enjoying each other's presence. Why was it sometimes painful for me? Most of my conversation was usually of the "problem-solving" variety. There was a problem. The group identified the problem. Then our conversation moved in an orderly fashion to shape an answer or a response.

This way of life reveals a high need to have control. Frankly, I struggle with the creation sagas in the first two chapters of the book of Genesis. I have wondered how long

God endured the chaos before God brought order. The different interpretations of how God brought life into being are not a big issue with me. How God tolerated the cosmic disorder before creation was my concern. God is God, and God can deal with more than I can. I know a little chaos would have driven me crazy.

So many of us go off to live our lives in expected, neat patterns and nice schemes. We tell ourselves and everyone else who will listen, "Plan your work and work your plan." We drive our families and friends crazy by saying, "There's a place for everything, and everything has its place." We live as if the nature of life is ordered, and, therefore, if we can discern the sequence, we can plan and prepare for everything.

People like me are ill prepared for experiences with grief. Our thought processes are clouded by emotions of fear, sadness, and anger. We lash out at the unexpected squall that has disrupted the tranquil waters we've learned to navigate.

Other people around us take control. Physicians walk into the hospital room and talk in an unfamiliar medical litany. Obviously, the doctors care about what is happening, but they have to maintain professional distance. Those of us who are part of the grief, however, don't have the distance. It's our child, our sibling, our parent whose life is on the line.

When we are in the hospital, we have to deal with interminable numbers of people with pink jackets and computers who ask for all our information and most importantly want to know if we have medical insurance. I know these are good people. Most of them are volunteers, but as we sit waiting for our turn to be seen, these folks chitchat and laugh about some funny thing one of their grandsons said.

Life has to be lived, but when we feel that we are losing a person or a relationship or we move from one season of life to another, we look for something to sustain us.

Things are out of my control. Life is not in my hands. I cry and ball up my fists in rage not only because someone I love is in incredible pain but also because I'm not in control, and I can't put Humpty Dumpty together again.

Order and Chaos

The book of Genesis relates the story of Adam and Eve's leaving the Garden of Eden. Eden was the place of order. "Adam and Eve," God said, "you name the animals." Basically, the ultimate Creator was saying, "You give identity to the rest of your world." When I name something or I identify where that something fits in the larger world, I control the world that surrounds me. I can put things where I want them. "Aardvarks are in front," I order. "Zebras, you go to the back." What I'm doing is systematizing my world. After all, "There is a place for everything, and everything has its place."

Yet, later readers and participants in the biblical saga knew that they didn't live in the Garden of Eden. Chaos and order struggled with each other, and people lived in a world where a woman named Sarai, who wanted to bear children, didn't conceive until she had arthritis and varicose veins. Brothers sold their sibling into slavery. Israel built temples and then watched them destroyed by nations who had no use for Israel's God. Jesus was crucified, others died for his cause, and churches that had such a promising start at Pentecost endured persecution.

"You are a serpent," Eve said. What Adam and she did not understand was that simply knowing the name didn't mean they understood the intention of everything and everyone. The garden in which they lived wasn't perfect. All may have seemed good, but all of us are about a piece of fruit's distance from being thrust into a world where a woman feels the pain of childbirth, and we all feel the pain of something.

In a profound sense, the saga of the Garden of Eden is a metaphor for life. We expect the ideal. We long for the order of Eden. We want to classify and systematize our worlds. Yet even in the purest of times, wily forces remind us in a split second that we are living in a world that is both sour and sweet. Somehow, some way, Eve and Adam had to leave the garden because the Hebrew people understood that much of life is lived outside Eden.

Outside the garden, grief and all sorts of unexpected things enter life. Cain kills his brother Abel. Why? Because Cain's sacrifice was not acceptable to God, and Abel's was. The sons of Adam and Eve became competitors; jealousy, envy, strife, and murder are suddenly a part of the fabric of existence. The Hebrews knew these painful qualities existentially, but they needed the story of how the best of humanity and the worst of humanity commingled. Goodness and badness, gain and loss, joy and grief—all of these were a part of existence.

Therefore, I write about grief, a common experience. By no means does this imply that all of our lives are lived in the valley of tears. Most of us know that life has incredible goodness. Everywhere I go I meet selfless, giving folks. I meet people who care deeply about their neighbors, their neighbor's daughter or son who goes off to war, and a world where force is too often the final arbiter.

These are people who go to their churches, synagogues, and mosques. They take food to people who are sick. They give to the poor, pray for peace, and rejoice when the young couple next door has a baby. When their families gather, they tell stories, laugh, and rejoice in the good things that have happened to each other. These people aren't cynics. They cry when something painful strikes someone they love, but they don't surrender themselves to a biting cynicism.

Most of these folks worship God. They may call the divine by different names, but they believe in a life force beyond themselves. They live out of the strength of their faith and express their gratitude for all of life's goodness.

These people are like many of us. While none of us chose to enter this world, we are grateful that we have the privilege to make this journey. As John Claypool, a minister who has influenced many of us, once said, "Life itself is a windfall." To be alive is a gracious gift, and many of us affirm this life as part of the benevolence of the Creator God.

Yet, we know that something is broken both within ourselves and within this world we inhabit. We respond to the brokenness with our grief. Some grief is expected. When my own father died, I was sad, but I also knew he had the gift of

ninety years. He would proudly tell people that he had two
sons, one a preacher and the other a lawyer. What made my
mother and him particularly proud was that neither of my
parents had completed high school. Both of them were
proud when Bob or I earned some degree and did what they
never had the chance to do.

When my father died, I would go to the telephone to
call him and realize that nobody would answer. I remember
when he would drive me to the first places where I preached.
I was too young for a driver's license and really too young to
be trying to tell anybody else how to live his life. On the way
home from preaching, my dad would gently offer his cri-
tique, which usually had to do with the sermon's being too
long.

While I grieved his death, I couldn't help being grateful
for the time he had with us and for his faith in God that
came later in my life but affected me with its genuineness.
These are the kinds of losses in life that we grieve, but we
understand that such dying is inevitable.

What concerns me more deeply are the painful changes
we experience that are inexplicable and unexpected. What
about lingering grief? What about a husband and a child
who are killed in an automobile accident, and the wife and
mother suddenly is without the man she loves most and the
daughter who was the delight of her life?

This happened to a former teaching colleague of mine.
All of us who know Deborah Carlton Loftis admire her not
only for the strong faith she has but also for the way she has
helped so many other people. Yet, which of us knows what
Deb thinks about in the silent moments of her life? Does she

think about the dreams she and her husband shared before he died too young? Does Deb wonder about her gifted daughter and everything the child may have become if she had the chance to become the beautiful woman she seemed destined to be?

I suppose one of the reasons I admire Deb is that she gives so much of herself to others even though so much has been taken from her. Nobody can explain why all of this has happened. We may reassure each other with the thought that the God of Christ prepares an eternal place for us. We may find in the dark night of our souls that there is strength for the next day, and the next, and the one after that. We will find solace in certain people who seem to understand the pain we can't put into words and who know better than to try to offer us quick fixes or pat answers.

The fact is that lingering grief demands a reorientation to the way we have done life. Since our son's diagnosis in 1983, our family has had to rethink the whole way we do life. As a minister, I have spent more hours than I can count attempting to understand how to recast both the words I speak to myself and the words I speak to others.

I am trying to learn how to live more faithfully in a world where the expectations I had for David won't be met. I struggle to accept what is rather than what I wish may have been. Perhaps, most of all, I am trying to be grateful for what is and especially who David is.

Sadness, anger, loneliness—these have been my traveling companions at times. What has helped me is to know that people who populate the Bible felt these feelings as well. Even Jesus! What must have surged through his heart when the disciples fell asleep the night before he died? What emotions did he face when he felt the anguish of the absence of his Heavenly Father even as he was heaving for breath?

The Absence of God

Perhaps most painful of all may have been the spiritual pain Jesus felt. We can understand better when somebody who doesn't like what we stand for wants to stop us, but what about Jesus' friends? According to John's Gospel, the disciples had followed Jesus for three years. These followers had listened to him, watched him, traveled with him, and yet, at the end of the journey, some of them exhibited astounding fear, self-centeredness, doubt, and even betrayal. At the table the night before his death, Jesus said that one of his closest followers would betray him. The disciples responded, "Is it I?" In other words, the potential of betraying the central thing in life exists in all of us.

One of the things that has helped in my own journey is to see the Bible as a document that reveals all facets of life. The Bible is not a "happily ever after" document. The shadow side of ourselves is revealed. Our emotions are on display. Seeing the "humanness" of the Bible doesn't make it any less inspiring or inspired. Rather, it reminds me again that the genius of God is the ability, as Jeremiah put it, to shape marred, flawed clay.

People in the Bible moved through the seasons of life. They also experienced their unique griefs. Even to encounter God was to open yourself to changes that you never expected and embark on a journey for which you had never planned.

As a minister, I never cease to be amazed at the common stories we share. Mention the word "grief" in a group, and people begin recalling details of their losses. We may be at different places in our healing, but we have a story of something or someone we are losing or we have lost. Some folks have taken a loved one to the cemetery, and others will look across the supper table at a child, a spouse, a parent who is still living, but they understand that something has changed, and it will never be as it used to be.

We are pilgrims together. We have much to learn from each other, and in the listening we may hear in a fresh way the caring voice of God.

Chapter Two

When Grief Becomes Personal

When Life Changes

None of us who was alive on September 11, 2001, will ever forget the tragedy of that day. Airplanes, commandeered by terrorists, crashed into the Twin Towers of the World Trade Center in New York City, the Pentagon in Washington D.C., and a mountainside in western Pennsylvania. Thousands of people were killed or injured. People lost daughters, sons, husbands, wives, and friends. All of us who lived in the United States lost any illusion that we were somehow immune from ethnic and religious hatred that filled the rest of the world.

We can speak generally about the chain of events that comprised 9/11, but those events involved the lives of individuals. A stock trader on the eightieth floor had a mother, maybe a husband, and two children who had gone to school that day expecting that their family would gather as usual around the dinner table that night. A priest, respected by the firefighters at the station where he served, would no longer be there to listen as a grizzled veteran of fighting fires talked about his sixteen-year-old daughter who seemed to be growing away from a dad who loved her with all his heart.

While grief is a common experience, it comes to us in personal ways. Books on grief can give us ideas about how to respond to loss and the emotions we experience. However, we are all built differently in the ways we process life and the ways we interpret our experiences.

For example, as long as I can remember, I have had a deep faith in God. While the way that I talk about God has changed with education and life experience, I have believed in a God whose nature was to love us. I believed in the "otherness" of God, but I also thought of God as a friend who cared about what happened to me. Prayer was the primary way to communicate my needs to God.

I understood that God wasn't in the business of responding to my self-centered wants. Even when I was in the throes of mid-life and thought a red sports car would help me forget the pain of joints that had not ached before, I would never have asked God for a flashy car. By the way, I never got a sports car with or without God. I have been a fan of the Miami Dolphins, but I didn't pray for Dan Marino to win a Super Bowl ring. Just as I didn't get the car, Dan Marino was never the quarterback on a team that won the Super Bowl. Maybe I should have prayed for the ring, the robe, and the red car. I've never liked sandals and venison, so I could have skipped the fatted calf.

However, I know that God had more important things to do than to root for me and my team. Children were starving; people were killing each other; domestic abuse was rampant; corporate greed was becoming a staggering problem. I had my own sins to confess. For example, what was I doing to help my small part of the world to be more humane, a kinder and more caring place?

All of this is to say that I function as a part of community. That community may be the world, the colleagues with whom I work, or my family as we sit around our table for a meal. I experience the joys and pains of these communities. Obviously, I don't feel each of these experiences as intensely as I do the pains and joys of those who are closest to me. Yet, when I watch the evening news and hear about a Palestinian child who has been killed in a bombing raid or an Israeli wife and mother who has been savagely wounded by a suicide bomber, I do feel for a least a few moments the connection that I have with others. I am not alone. Yet, you and I are alone in a profound sense. When grief breaks into our lives, all that we are and all that has shaped us become our resources to deal with the sadness.

When our son was diagnosed with his tumor, I saw things about myself that either helped me to accept what had happened or at times kept me from moving on with the new reality of David's life or the different kind of future we faced. I will try to name these things with the prayer that what is most personal is also most universal. May you who read these words find meaning in them.

The Need to Control

The first night after the tumor had been identified, I recall sitting with my wife and several doctors as the medical people told us what we were facing and outlined our possi-

ble choices. It all seemed surreal. We were still reeling from
the unexpected news that David had a brain tumor. We were
afraid, tired, struggling to gain our footing. Life had flipped
upside down, and now physicians were speaking a strange
language in what for me was a foreign land. The psalmist
asked, "How can we sing a new song in an alien land?" My
question was, "How can I even understand what others are
singing and saying in this place called a hospital?"

The words of the doctors seemed flat, as if they were dis-
cussing something in which none of them had any
significant personal investment. When I was a student at
seminary, I remember our pastoral care professors telling
future ministers how we needed to maintain a balance
between intimacy and distance. "Let people feel your
warmth," they said, "but be far enough away so that when
they come to you, they feel they've come some distance."

About a year after I had been at my first pastorate, a
small rural church just the right size for a seminary student,
I learned that two leaders in the church were having an
extramarital affair. It sent devastating waves through that
congregation. Members of the church were angry, sad, and
disappointed. Some people wondered if the church could
survive such trauma. Not only were people concerned about
the folks and families involved, but also they wondered if
the image of the church could ever be restored in our southern Indiana community.

As pastor, I felt I was at the epicenter of this trauma. I
felt responsible to hold the church together. At the same
time, I was experiencing my own anger and sadness. The
people involved were my friends. They were respected lead-

ers of our congregation. I had no inkling of what was happening between these church leaders until the problem erupted. To use the metaphor of Father Henri Nouwen, I saw myself as the "wounded healer." The problem was that my own wounds were so deep, and I had little to offer others as a healer.

I went to see one of my seminary professors for advice. Swan Haworth was a wise and compassionate person. He listened; he cared for me; he offered me words of encouragement. However, what I remember most is what he did at the end of our conversation. Dr. Haworth had an office with a window that looked out on Lexington Road, a busy road that ran in front of the seminary campus. "Suppose," my professor said as he called me to look out the window at Lexington Road, "there was an automobile accident in front of the seminary. An injured person was lying in the street. You raced out to help. But instead of helping, you sat by the injured person and simply said, 'I want to be injured with you.'"

My professor understood my pain, but he was teaching me a valuable lesson. Those of us in ministry must have some separation from those to whom we minister. To care for somebody doesn't mean to get sick with her. We try to love people. We want to care for them. But if we personally walk through every valley, we will have short ministries and little to offer others as help.

As the parade of pediatricians, neurosurgeons, and other doctors walked in and out of my family's life, I had the distinct feeling that some of them had developed distance very well. Of course there were exceptions. Some of our doctors shared care for us in ways that let us know that what happened to David and what we were experiencing were important to them.

Yet, no physician despite his or her competency or care could give a precise prognosis. We constantly faced medical crossroads. The doctors presented us options for treatment. They shared the risks of each procedure. Diane and I were signing documents that included a litany of things that could go wrong in a surgery or a treatment. Perhaps most poignant for our family were the times we kissed our son as David was being taken to surgery. We went back to the waiting room, aptly named because there we sat, prayed, and hoped but mostly waited to hear about our child.

"Wait on the Lord," the Old Testament prophet admonishes his listeners. I suppose it had never dawned on me what those words meant for the way in which we are forced at times to live. Waiting on the Lord is a striking statement of faith in a God who moves in God's own ways and for God's purposes. From our side, it reminds those of us who are the created ones that we don't shape all the contours of our existence. We work to do our best, and we work to make happen what we believe is best for those whom we love. We wait, however, on the Lord and are reminded in the process that we are finite and limited.

The Need to Understand

If I finally realize that I'm not in charge and in control of the universe, then the next best thing is the ability to understand

and articulate the reasons for something that seems so unreasonable. Theologians often speak about the power to "name" something. If I can name the evil, then I may be able to describe it and give others and myself the satisfaction of an explanation. Most of us have been trained to think logically. If we can't control suffering, at least we can name it and explain it in a way that makes sense.

Many of us who are ministers want desperately to make sense of the sadness we encounter. I was still a student in college when I officiated at my first funeral. A baby had died. The family was devastated. I don't recall everything I said, but I think I said something about the way life makes sense from God's perspective, and certainly God had some purpose for all of this pain.

The family politely thanked me for my remarks, but I went home from that service berating myself for being so presumptuous. I wish I could say that was the last time that I presumed to know God's purposes. Unfortunately, presumption about the mystery of the divine and the mysteries of living seems to be a vocational hazard of some of us who are ministers.

As I watched David face what none of us had ever expected, it dawned on me that so much of what people encounter defies explanation. In my own fatigue and fear, I scrambled in my mind to name a reason. Was it something I had done or not done? Was it a sin of the father that had set his son's life on edge?

God knows I had sinned, but if David's illness was caused by something I had done or left undone, it all seemed unfair and out of proportion. What kind of God was this, anyway? If God was causing this to happen to make me depend more on God, this made no sense. In fact, at the moment I most needed God, I felt an enormous barrier between God and me.

As I have looked back at those times when our family moved through the darkest stretches of the valley, I realize how vulnerable I was in trying to make some sense of the suffering. Maybe pain does that to many of us. It dislodges us from our theological moorings. It sets us adrift in a sea of questions, often asking, "What have I done to deserve this?" or "Why did this happen to me?"

We see the effects, and then we try to reason our way back to the cause. Surely something I had read in a book or studied when I was in theological school would provide the clue. You and I throw a stone into the lake, and we watch the ripples of the water move toward us as we stand at the edge. The ripples are the effect. The rock is the cause. This makes sense.

Yet, when we read the Bible, we are confronted with so much that is beyond sense or above sense or seems to make no sense. The waters are parted, they churn, they are calmed, and we keep looking for the stone that set all this in motion. If we can name the stone, then we can make sense of what looks to be chaotic and confusing.

For all of us, some order to life is important. We want to understand so that we can put some form around the formless or give reasons for what seems unreasonable. For some of us, that need to have order is insatiable. Perhaps it is a result of our family history, our life experiences, or the way we are "mapped" by our own DNA.

Whatever the reasons, I am part of that group of people who likes to have the "dots connected." I don't like chaos or confusion. "A place for everything and everything in its place" is my mantra. What I want for my life, I also want for the world in which I live. Recently, a friend shared with me that he was being treated for malignant tumors. As with many cancers, his had metastasized. The cancer had spread, and the doctors had given him radiation and chemotherapy. Still, the tumors were present in his lungs and in several other organs. "We'll wait to see if you begin to have difficulty breathing," the physicians said, "and then we'll try to address the symptoms.

My friend is a relatively young man. He has children and grandchildren. He will probably never live to see all his grandchildren graduate from kindergarten. How does he handle it? Gracefully. Graciously. Grateful for the days that he is given to see another sunset or to read a story to a grandchild who doesn't understand that all the stories of life don't finish with "and they all lived happily forever."

Those of us who know this man are enriched by his life but also wonder why he won't have his "threescore and ten." He is a genuinely good person. He is a Christian, so he lives with the hope of resurrection and reunion. Yet, we need more of his kind with us in this world. He's kind and gentle. He is a peacemaker in the place where he lives. In a word, he embodies love. Why is he the one to be taken from us too soon?

Edmund Steimle, the outstanding Lutheran minister, used to ask, "Why are ministers the last to understand that life doesn't always have symmetry?" Steimle, who also taught

preaching, was reacting to all the sermons he had heard that
ended with a problem solved and the rough edges of experience rounded off.

Of course, Steimle is right. Sermons become thin gruel
when those of us who preach cannot live with the questions
and pretend we have answers that we don't. Yet, preachers
with pat answers may have been responding to listeners like
me who wanted to believe that life was always fair and bal-
anced. We wanted to believe not only that God was good
but also that God was good to those of us who try in our
own ways to be as good as we can.

When David became so ill, it knocked my sense of the
fairness of life for a loop. The symmetrical way in which I
connected good with goodness was shattered. I couldn't
order this new reality in the old categories that had shaped
my frame of reference.

Jesus speaks of the inability to put new wine into old
wineskins. While Jesus was speaking about the new life that
he was bringing, his metaphor can also be used to help us
understand those times when new realities can't be con-
tained in old perceptions. What do we do in those
moments?

We can deny the new reality or try to escape its pain. I
did think about that. What would it be like if I abandoned
my responsibilities to my family and just left? What if I put
as much physical distance between the pain and my presence? If I didn't have to face the situation each day, perhaps I
could turn painful reality into a distant memory.

I didn't book passage on a ship to the other side of the
world, but denial and escape were attractive options. Fleeing

the scene of a son's suffering may seem like the ultimate act of self-centeredness, and, of course, it is selfishness. However, to face the beast every day savages our best judgment and makes us want to find some relief.

In fall 2004, I audited a class with Dr. Ronald Heifetz at the John F. Kennedy School of Government at Harvard University. Heifetz writes and teaches about leadership. He spoke about "work avoidance." Any effective leader knows that before a problem can be solved, it needs to be admitted and named. Work avoidance may take the form of denial or even infantile escapism. Which of us hasn't faced a complex problem and said, "If I don't deal with it, maybe it will just go away" or "Maybe the problem will just solve itself"?

When my children were young, they used to shut their eyes if something in their world was threatening. What they were doing is what we all wish we could do at times—if I pretend not to see the problem, the problem won't be there. When I open my eyes, everything in front of me will be as I want.

Unfortunately, this is wishful thinking. Unless we just have a penchant for conflict, we don't go around looking for confrontation. However, avoidance is a form of denial.

The Suffering of Jesus

For those of us who are Christians, the consummate act of not avoiding pain is Jesus' choice to die. Interestingly, the thought of a different path seems to have crossed Jesus' mind. In the Garden of Gethsemane, Jesus asked for the possibility of some way through Gethsemane and around Golgotha.

Unlike some Christians who wear their sacrifices for faith as badges of honor, Jesus verbalized the kind of honesty that many of us feel. Suffering for Jesus or for anything meaningful may come, but it's not a guest that we warmly welcome. Watching people we love suffer may help us to become more sensitive and caring, but surely sensitivity and caring don't have to be learned in such a demanding and draining classroom.

Frankly, I find Jesus' confession, "If there be any other way, let this cup pass from me," to be true to the way I pray. I like to think that I can deal with pain, that I don't run from it or avoid it at all costs. At the same time, I don't awaken in the morning asking God to give me a cross to test my spiritual meddle.

However, Jesus' reluctance to move to the place of excruciating suffering did not cause him to resist it. He didn't remain in Gethsemane or flee to the safety of Galilee. What turned the final days of Jesus' earthly life into an act of redemption were his words to the Heavenly Father: "Yet not my will but thine be done."

I recognize the fundamental difference between what Jesus did and what others of us have to face. He chose this road. He summoned the courage to say "yes" to suffering when he seemed to have the option to say "no." Jesus took up the cross, his cross, and carried it to the brutal end because he sensed that all of this was a part of God's redemptive plan.

While Jesus chose his suffering, most of us experience suffering that chooses us. Recently, I spoke at a meeting in Birmingham, Alabama. The time coincided with the fortieth anniversary of the civil rights march to Selma, Alabama. Many of those interviewed on television and in newspaper articles had participated in the original march. Their belief in the equality of all God's children made them choose to face water hoses, police dogs, time in jail, and the taunts of people who were tethered to a segregated way of life they had always known.

The Choice of Suffering

The marches to Selma had a redemptive purpose even if it meant personal pain. People like Martin Luther King Jr., John Lewis, and countless others knew they had a great purpose even if it meant great cost. Whatever reluctance they may have had to encounter those who despised them or who did not understand why things had to change was overcome by their conviction that the time for redemption and racial reconciliation had come.

Suffering that chooses us does not come with an obvious redemptive purpose. You and I are thrust into a valley, and we don't know how far and wide and long the journey is. We have the sense that our lives and the lives of those we love will never be the same. What we don't know is how this will change us or whether we will ever be able to put our suffering into some larger redemptive purpose.

At that point, we have choices to make. These are life-changing choices. What has happened is fact. How we respond becomes a statement of our faith or lack of faith. How do we respond when we can't explain why something has happened? As children of enlightenment, we search for reasons as if explanation is sufficient strength for any valley through which we walk. Why did this happen to my son, to my family, to any child, or to any family? All we hear is the echo of our question.

The choice is to live or not to live. Or to say it another way, how do we choose to live? What I have decided is that I will always live with some questions. On this side of eternity, those questions will never be fully answered. I live with wounds. I imagine what may have been had this tumor never touched my son. Would he make some noble contribution to life? Would he marry? Would his wife and he give us more grandchildren that his mother and I could spoil shamelessly without ever feeling the slightest twinge of shame? I don't know.

What I do know is that David has taught us more about the virtues of life than I think I would have learned if this had never happened. I see his quiet faith in God. I have watched David's courage as he has been forced to march through his own valley of the shadow of death. I wonder at his insight into people's feelings and the ability to say the most sensitive things in only a few words. He didn't get that from his minister father, who says a lot but often is embarrassed by how little a lot of my words can really say. Most of all, I'm moved by his love for a rescued dog who doesn't know how good she has it . . . and for his love for a family who loves him with all of our hearts.

I don't understand. I do understand. I suppose it is like, "O God, I believe; help my unbelief." When grief becomes personal, we understand as never before that life is complex and faith in God does not preclude the fears that sometimes fill our lives.

Chapter Three

When Grief Seems to Have No End

Living with Reality

Our local Richmond, Virginia, newspaper carried a moving story about an American soldier who had returned home from Iraq. When he went to Iraq, he was healthy with a seemingly bright future. One day while stationed near Baghdad, a roadside bomb hit his vehicle. While the young soldier lived, the trauma he suffered to his head left him with cognitive deficits, confusion, and depression. The soldier was undergoing rehabilitation. "All I want," he said, "is to be the person that I was before."

His family expressed love and support for him. A person of deep faith, his mother said, "We will welcome him as he is and realize that the fact that he is living is a blessing."

The mother's words moved me deeply. While our son wasn't injured in combat, David did suffer irreparable damage. In many ways, he is not the same child we knew for the first ten years of his life.

Our family is grateful that David is alive. In my best moments, he reminds me that each moment we have is a sheer gift from God. When he and I sit in the family room to watch a favorite television show, I remember that I can hug him, embrace him, or simply glance out of the corner of my eye at the son I still have.

I never want to seem ungrateful. As a minister, I have done too many funeral services for parents who yearn for one more embrace. Yet, the words of that young American soldier haunt me, "All I want is to be the person that I was before."

Probably, that young soldier will never be that person. The type of injury he suffered has done permanent damage. With rehabilitation, he may recover some of his mental functioning. With therapy and proper medication, he may be able to overcome some of his debilitating depression. However, the fact is that he will live all of his life with the consequences of a moment in time that changed every subsequent moment of time that he has.

When his family and he are together, they will have moments of joy and gratitude, but they see a son whose life is altered, and all of them will be altered in the process.

Living with Grief and Gratitude

Perhaps grief and gratitude are not opposites. They may be responses to life that we will experience, and sometimes we will experience them at the same moment. Several years ago, I was an interim pastor of a church that was moving through the Lenten season. When I was growing up, I heard no mention of Lent in my home church. In fact, I wouldn't have known what the word "Lent" meant if it wasn't for my friend Danny. Danny and his family were Roman Catholics. I always envied Danny because he didn't have to attend church as much as I did as a Baptist. Besides, his worship service was conducted in Latin so he didn't know much of what was happening anyway.

However, during Lent Danny seemed to become more serious about his faith. He had to give up something. I don't recall that Danny made any great sacrifices. One year he gave up attending movies. Another year, I think he abstained from chocolate. Danny assured me, however, that when Lent was over, he could pick up where he had left off.

That was my childhood perspective of Lent. My own Christian faith had ordinary times as well as Easter moments. The concept of the Christian faith as an uneven journey was missing. I relished the thrill of Christmas and Easter but thought the rest of what we experienced in the church was a prelude to the stories of gift and triumph.

Perhaps this contributed to my own faith that saw the presence of God in the extraordinary but saw little of God in the ordinary or in the difficult. When David became ill, I saw little of God's presence. In my family's life, it hardly felt like Christmas or Easter.

How do we deal with those times of personal Lent when we journey through desert and darkness? If we can't explain, how do we find some way to interpret those times when we feel the tomb is still sealed, and our hope is sealed with it?

Living the Questions

As a minister, I am asked to give a theological framework in which people can try to interpret their pain. I remember funeral services for people who had committed suicide. I was speaking into the teeth of the unfortunate notion that suicide was the unpardonable sin. While the Bible does not support this idea, we all know how prevalent it is.

In addition, family members and friends of the deceased were left with a multiplicity of emotions. "Why didn't I notice the signs of distress?" "Why did my husband leave me with children, and now I have to try to make sense to them of something I don't understand myself?"

No minister can bring words that even begin to touch the hem of the garment of these deep questions. However, the minister does seek to bring reassurance that suicide is not the unpardonable sin. Maybe the minister tries to help the family understand that depression isn't just a spiritual problem. Each of us is wired differently, and, for some, that means each step of life is more difficult than many of us will ever understand.

As ministers, we strive to give ourselves and others a more realistic framework for seeing life. We acknowledge that life is both death and aliveness, both arduous journeys through rugged hills and winding roads as well as joyous births. A mother groans as a child is born, and then she smiles as her son's face meets hers for the first time.

When grief broke into our family's life, it was an unwelcome, despised guest who took over our home and brought a gloom that filled every corner of our being. This grief seemed antithetical to an understanding of the Christian faith seen only through the Sundays of Christmas and Easter.

As some of the numbness and shock of David's illness began to lift, I tried to find an interpretative framework for myself both as a father and a minister. I knew there had been a seismic shift in the geography of our family's life. I also knew that the shadow of David's suffering would cast itself across the days and nights ahead of us. Things were irreparably changed. There was no closure and no finality. Whenever we saw David, we would be reminded of the gift of his life, but we would also see a son whose existence had been sliced cruelly into before and after.

At one and the same time, our family would be grateful, but we would also grieve. How then do we live? I suppose for the first time it dawned on me how powerful our choices are. Something happens. How do we respond? We experience change, and the question is, "How do we react when life tilts in an unexpected direction?"

The Example of Jesus

There are texts in the Bible that help us to be more alive to the life-altering choices Jesus made. In Luke's Gospel, Jesus' first sermon at his hometown synagogue in Nazareth is met with extraordinary hostility. In fact, the townsfolk want to throw Jesus off a cliff. Yet, Jesus walks through the crowd and proceeds to Capernaum, where he offers the gift of himself.

s seems to model the notion of life as a journey. His journey here was filled with rejection, but Jesus chose to move on. There's no suggestion in Luke's account that rejection in his hometown froze Jesus either physically or emotionally. Surely that rejection must have stung. Yet, Jesus did not live looking backward to the time when the reaction to him was violence. He moved forward to do what needed to be done and to say what needed to be said.

In John's Gospel, much emphasis is placed on Jesus' turning his face toward Jerusalem. The disciples knew what that meant. Not only was Jesus choosing the "via dolorosa," but also he was inviting his followers to choose the way of suffering.

This was the "passion" of Jesus. On the other side of Gethsemane and Golgotha were resurrection and the conquest of death. But before the empty tomb, there needed to be a dead body. We can't have a resurrection without a crucifixion. No wonder the disciples resisted the "passion of Jesus." Unless we are masochistic, we usually don't choose to put our lives in the hands of those who want to hurt us.

Yet, this is what Jesus did. Crucified . . . buried . . . raised on the third day! This has been the historic affirmation of the church. The church has said that Jesus is both victim and victor. Jesus is "Christus Victor" and "Christus Victim." Jesus suffered. Jesus died. Thank God for Easter Sunday morning, but the only way to celebrate the brightness of the new day is to acknowledge the darkness of a few days before.

Our own lives reflect both the darkness and the light. On this side of eternity, both grace and grief are our companions. Even the most optimistic person has to admit that optimism is a wonderful attitude, but it hardly makes pain disappear. Optimism is an "in spite of" attitude.

Perhaps realism is a more biblical attitude, or at least one that reflects who Jesus was. Grief pursued him all the days of his earthly life. Did his mother and half-brothers and half-sisters understand him or his ministry? Mostly not. Was he rejected? Yes. Was he deserted? Yes. Did he experience my kind of loss? Certainly.

Did Jesus have a sense of purpose? Yes. Was he joyful? Jesus spoke often of "blessedness," and he told stories about people who gave lavish parties when a lost something or someone was found. Did Jesus laugh? Hyperbole is probably not our favorite form of humor, but the idea of a camel going through the eye of the needle may have drawn a few first-century chuckles.

The point is that Jesus experienced all of life and reflected that in his precepts and presence. At the risk of sounding too flippant, we may say Jesus was authentic, the real deal! Pursued by goodness and mercy, Jesus showed us how to live when we are also pursued by badness and madness.

As dean of the divinity school at Gardner-Webb University, I teach one course a semester. Like each member of the faculty, I'm evaluated every semester by the students. The students give us scores of 1-5 on ten components of our teaching. One of those areas of evaluation asks, "Is the professor fair and reasonable?" I like to think of myself as fair and reasonable, so I give myself a "5." Would you believe that not every one of my students has given me a perfect score? Of course, the students don't sign their names. So mentally I have to go through the class rolls and try to figure out who's not seeing me as being always fair and reasonable.

I try to rationalize. Probably, I remind the student of some teacher he didn't like, and what we have is a classic case of "transference." She didn't appreciate something her home church pastor said, and what am I teaching? It's called preaching, and she gave me this grade that she would like to have given to her pastor.

Life Is Not Always Fair

Of course, when I finally get over the illusion that I'm perfect, I understand that most of the students are more gracious to me than I deserve. After all, "fairness" is in the eye of the beholder. When I play with my grandson, I'm told, "Grampa, you're not being fair." I think I'm being more than fair. But unless everything is happening exactly the way Finn wants, it's certainly not his fault. It must be Grampa's problem.

In a powerful sermon, Barbara Brown Taylor tells us we had better be grateful that God doesn't play fair. She uses the parable of the workers who are hired one hour before quitting time and who are paid first, receiving the same wages as those who have worked all day. It's a parable that sometimes I wish Jesus hadn't told. When I have preached from this text, only a few adults who were baptized in the last year like the sermon. The chair of the nominating committee says on her way out the door, "Let's hold off on that parable until we

get all the committees filled!" She's right! Unless we're
workaholics or riddled with guilt when we try to relax, we're
going to start late, get paid first, and have the same amount
of money to spend at the store.

Barbara Brown Taylor's message is that the grace of God
isn't fair, and we need to thank God because none of us
deserves the gift. Can we also say that grief, even the grief
that never ends, can also be a gift? Is it possible to write a
song, "Amazing Grief"? Can the loss we experience remind
us that life isn't fair? Who told us that it would always be
"fair and reasonable" as we define those terms? Or can we
even say that grief reminds us that we are all at a "loss" to
explain why we received what we think we don't deserve,
both good and bad?

How tricky this business of theodicy is. Why do seemingly innocent people suffer? Why is a bright, winsome
young theologian, father, and husband diagnosed with MS?
Why do we see small children afflicted with AIDS or starve
to death or become victims of genocide simply because they
are born in the wrong place to parents who are themselves
victims?

I don't have the answers, just as I didn't have the answer
when my son was diagnosed. The results of his illness are
reflected in his face, his limbs, his scarred head, his mind,
and they are an unspoken part of every conversation we
have. The effects of the tumor and the treatments remind all
of our family of the day life took a vicious turn for us.

Grief and Sensitivity

The grief goes on! Time and the grace of God give those of us who love David dearly some distance from the intensity of those first years when we struggled to give our child the help he needed and wrestled with the question of why. Yet, here is the most remarkable part of this journey: David has shown all of us the strength to endure and the courage to live when the rest of us felt as if we were dying on the inside.

David understands that he is different now in many ways. He becomes frustrated. He knows that the puzzle books he enjoys have to be in large print because his sight has been affected. David understands that his lack of energy keeps him from doing some things that require stamina. David recognizes that he will always need somebody to care for him and to make sure he takes his medications and that some structure and order are given to his life.

David is aware that the rest of his life will be set largely by his limits. Yet, in a way that is remarkable to all of us who know him, he faces the future with a faith that inspires us. Our son is very quiet. He doesn't talk much about what's on his mind and in his heart. But his simple acts of kindness and thoughtfulness to others are staggering reminders that he hasn't retreated within himself, and David reminds me and others who know him that caring for people is actually a challenge to live our own lives with deeper sensitivity.

Perhaps David would have this compassion if there had never been a tumor. While I'm biased as his dad and feel that regardless of what had happened, my son would be caring about others, I can't help believing that his own suffering has given him a capacity to care and an ability to empathize that far exceeds mine.

For example, David and I have been with people in a group. That's not David's favorite thing. He will respond when somebody talks to him, but he seldom initiates conversation. On the other hand, David's father usually talks too much and listens too little. This gives rise to some interesting conversations when he and I are riding home together. "Did you notice, Dad . . . ?" and then David will call the name of someone who was especially quiet or who never laughed when all the other people were enjoying themselves.

I realize that they don't award a Nobel Prize for such an act of presence and concern, but wouldn't the world be a better place if our lives weren't so cluttered or if we weren't so busy trying to be the center of attention that we often overlook those who need our attention?

When grief seems to have no end, the person with Down's Syndrome reminds us that exuberant, expressive love is such a gift. The man whose wife wants a divorce shows that even in the midst of human rejection, divine acceptance can give us the strength to move on with life. Do these kinds of responses to loss happen every time? Of course not. Even the ways some of us respond to small setbacks make us aware how easy it is to clench our fists and teeth and stay angry, bitter, and cynical.

However, there are enough people to remind us that lingering grief may have a different "end." That end or purpose may be to let us know that a person's attitude may overcome the situation. Do circumstances, as difficult as they may be, dictate the way we respond to life, or can the grace of God turn grief into "amazing grief"?

To say that I see God in David is an understatement. When I look at my son, I see gentleness, kindness, peace, love, patience, joy exhibited in a son who relishes the gift of existence. I see a quiet faith in God that speaks more eloquently than any words I ever shape.

I wouldn't be honest if I didn't say that sometimes I look at David and think, "What may have been?" But that question is already answered. Now the questions are, "What is?" and "How will we respond to what is the given of our child's life?" If it is given, then it is a gift. Certainly not the gift I would have chosen. However, some of the best gifts I've ever received were not what I would have chosen. For David and the gift of his life, I say, "Thanks be to God!"

Chapter Four

When God Appears to Grow Silent

In summer 1969, I prepared one of my most difficult sermons. I was doing a Clinical Pastoral Education unit at the Central State Hospital in LaGrange, Kentucky. Central was the state mental hospital for Kentucky.

Before the days of community mental health centers, Central State was a conglomeration of warehouse-type buildings housing psychiatric patients with all kinds of conditions. When I walked into a "locked" unit and introduced myself as the chaplain, I was met with myriad reactions. Most ignored me. A few told stories that made little sense to me. For example, one woman kept telling me about a camp in southern Indiana that housed German prisoners during World War II. Several were openly hostile and eviscerated me with words when I tried to enter their private worlds with words of my own.

During the summer, each of the students had to prepare and deliver a sermon. Our teachers were insistent about our remembering that many of the patients interpreted words in a highly literal way and concretized figurative language. The supervisors reminded us that words for a song such as "In the Garden"—"God walks with me, and he talks with me, and he tells me I am his own"—were an example of how metaphorical language would be heard in a literal way.

Granted, most preachers don't have to exercise this much care in considering the way words are heard. In fact, some ministers who like to pepper their sermons with images, illustrations, and inductions can hardly conceive of an audience that listens only at a literal level. We assume a preaching style that traces itself to Jewish rabbis and to Jesus himself. After all, didn't Jesus employ stories, metaphors, and similes? Didn't Jesus invite hearers to draw mental pictures of a prodigal child, a father's goodness, and a Samaritan woman who was invited to drink "living water"? Information alone wasn't the goal of Jesus' teaching. He seemed to be trying to stir those deep places in all of us where we remember in images and stories.

However, all of us who preach struggle with the gap between what we are trying to say and what people hear. We want to give people room to create meaning for themselves, but if their meanings bear no resemblance to our messages, then we have a communication problem.

How Does God Speak?

With this in mind, I want to ask, "Does God have a communication problem?" Or does God speak clearly, and we should hear clearly, and if we just had enough faith or trust, there would be no problem? An old bumper sticker captured the perceived certainty of human-divine communication:

"God said it; I believe it; and that settles it." Conversation over!

I know there are people who live their faith this way, and in some sense I envy them. They deal with the "ups and downs" of life and believe God is with them and speaking to them through all their experiences. It's simple arithmetic, and I don't want to diminish the trust these people have in God. We all need ballast in our lives, and it's hardly my job to be telling folks that their coping devices are too simplistic.

Yet, some of us know that as much as we may like, we are not able to live at that level. It's not that we're brighter or more informed, but we're not able to see or hear God so clearly in the complexities of our lives. I love simple arithmetic. In fact, I still remember when our math teacher taught us short division. As far as I was concerned, we didn't have to go any further. But the teacher said we had to learn long division and do problems that covered a whole sheet of paper and required decimal points in the answers.

Then it was something more complex until one day in college I said, "That's it for me. I've passed the required math courses. I'm on my way to history, English, and the other parts of the curriculum that are more congenial to my interests."

So please understand. I'm not against simplicity. In fact, when I teach preaching, I often cite William Muehl, former homiletics professor at Yale. Muehl drew a distinction between vulgar simplification and profound simplicity. Good preaching isn't the minister's using words that people don't understand or talking about ideas that are disconnected from the issues our listeners face. But neither is preaching, as Muehl contends, the minister's claiming that if she hurls enough clichés at the congregation, that will supply easy answers to difficult questions.

What do we say if we aren't going to say something that sounds like "vulgar simplification"? First, does God speak? Not nearly as clearly or as loudly as I would like! I've never heard God say anything to me in the same way that I hear my wife. Some of the writers in the Bible believe strongly that God speaks, and creative, transforming things happen. The words of God have power to shape and reshape. Worlds are brought into being through the words of the Holy One who desires to create other life that God can love.

I believe this. I believe in the God of the Bible who wants to restore a relationship that is broken. I believe I am broken and the world in which I live is broken. I know what I can say to someone whom I love that is cruel and heartless. I see the brokenness of the world around me. Too many people are dying of hunger or of AIDS. Our demand for oil and gasoline seems boundless, and we are choking the life out of a world whose ecosystem we have made dysfunctional.

Does God want better from you and me? Does God want us to be more caring and compassionate? Or, to put it another way, does God want us to know that God cares when we face some overwhelming problem? I'm going to answer "Yes," but it's a qualified yes.

God doesn't speak as clearly as I would like. God seems to whisper, or if God is saying anything, about all I hear is, "Endure it and perhaps learn something from your endurance." What I really want God to say about my son and maybe your son or anybody's child is "I'll fix the problem, and then you will know I really love you."

In a church where I'm interim pastor, I've met a man who is gentle and quiet. Nobody seems to be more respected in this church than he. One Wednesday evening I sat with him as we finished supper. The rest of the people began to leave, and we had a few minutes before prayer meeting.

"I've heard you mention David," Larry said. "I can identify with you." And then Larry told me the story of his younger brother. Shortly after birth, Larry's brother contracted polio. It left him unable to walk. "For years," Larry shared, "my brother lived with my parents. My mother and dad made sure that all of his needs were met." Finally, they reached the age when they were unable to care for him. The family decided that he needed to be in a nursing home. After his parents' deaths, Larry assumed the caretaker's role for his brother. "I visit him several times a week. He and I like to watch the Atlanta Braves' baseball games," Larry said with that shy grin of his.

"How did your folks respond to the illness of your brother?" I asked.

"I never heard them complain," Larry said. Of course, I'd never met Larry's parents, but suddenly I had this mental picture of a man and woman hearing that one of their two children would never walk again and deciding that they would accept it and deal with a reality they never expected.

The serenity prayer first spoken by theologian Reinhold Niebuhr and reshaped across the years reminds us that part of living is finding strength that will help us accept the things we cannot change. Of course, the other part of that prayer is summoning the courage to change the things we can and to find in God the wisdom to know what we have to accept and what we can help to change.

"I never heard my parents complain," Larry told me, and I saw in Larry himself the same strength. While his brother suffered from the debilitating effects of polio and lived in a nursing home, Larry smiled as he shared with me the story of the two brothers watching their favorite baseball team on television. I never had the sense that anybody felt like a helpless victim—not Larry, not his parents, not even his brother. After all, what really mattered in the moment was a baseball team, a game, and two brothers who shared a passion for the Atlanta Braves.

Interestingly, the name of God never entered Larry's and my conversation. Nobody said, "This is God's will," "God allowed my brother to get polio," or even "God is using this bad situation to effect some good." In fact, using these kinds of phrases would have lessened the impact of what was said. This was a family whose faith in God was deep and who displayed that faith in the way they responded, not through words that would have sounded vacuous.

This family had accepted what was. Larry recalled, "My mom and dad never questioned God." Paul Tullich would have said these people "adjusted to what would not adjust to them." Did the parents ever express any lament to God? Did the younger brother ever question why he couldn't walk? Did Larry ever secretly wish as a boy that he didn't have to answer questions like, "What's wrong with your brother?"

I don't know if anybody in the family ever cried, became angry, or wondered why polio struck their family. From what I know about Larry, my hunch is that if any of these responses occurred, they were only momentary. Some people find strength to accept uneven movements of life because they understand that life itself is uneven. To expect God to even the highway and to make our journeys smooth is to expect God to do what God has never promised.

Yet, accepting what we can't change seems like weakness to some of us. In my own life, I have seen myself needing to make a difference. Perhaps it's part of my own need to justify my existence. My self-esteem is tied too closely to what I can do to effect change. As a pastor, I remember how important it was to me for the church to grow and to do well. Did I do this for Jesus' sake? I hope part of my motivation was for something beyond me. However, I know my own fear of failure. To be told that I needed to accept things as they were was tantamount to personal failure.

Reminded of Our Limits

Dealing with a loss in our lives is a reminder of our limits. Throughout David's experience, I've been reminded of my helplessness. So often I wanted to make things different, but no amount of desire on my part has turned loss into gain. I can't work or will brokenness into wholeness. Either I learn to accept what can't be changed, or I go crazy trying to change what is beyond my capacity.

Does God work in helping us to accept what can't be changed? As a child, I wondered why God didn't fix what I thought was broken. When I started preaching, I thought,

"Why doesn't everybody change to the kind of person I am calling her or him to be?" Later, when my reasoning caught up with my rhetoric, I realized that I wasn't often being and doing what I glibly called others to be and do.

The serenity prayer reminds us that part of the power to live is to ". . . accept what we cannot change." In accepting what we can't change about ourselves or others, we face the limits of our humanity. We recognize our boundaries. In a theological sense, we begin to understand our need for something or someone beyond ourselves.

That recognition brings both pain and possibilities. The pain is acknowledging that not only are we not God, but also we also don't understand all the ways in which God works. We may try to mask our private pain by pretending that we are in control and that we are adequate for each and every situation. Of course, we know differently, but the temptation to appear to others as invulnerable or as having the capacity to explain the inexplicable are tempting. We avoid the vulnerability that opens us to others and to the fact that both others and ourselves understand our limits.

The pain of acknowledging our limits is part of the reason for the rise of religious fundamentalism throughout our world. People in authority speak with authority, and they shape a world that seems symmetrical and ordered. Answers to difficult questions are easily articulated, and the attraction for us is that all ambiguity is eliminated. We live from one certainty to another certainty, and mystery is replaced by the conviction of those who have the answers.

The difficulty with this ambiguity is replaced, and the recognition of our own humanity is eliminated, by the need to have a corner on all truth. No longer do we see through a glass darkly. Right thinking about God replaces relationship with God, and we lose the beauty of a love that grows in its understanding of the other but is always surprised by what we discover in the beloved.

The Grace of God on the Journey

That's the possibility of confessing our humanity and our limits. The grace of God calls us to a journey where God is both with us and beyond us. God is our companion as well as our destination. I want to know about God, but mostly, I want to know God better. I want to keep looking through the dark glass and to be surprised by any gracious glimpses of this Holy One.

If you and I can live like this, we may find a new way to listen for God or even to understand that God is at work when from our side the Divine One seems silent. I pray for God's will. I pray for my will. When God responds the way I want, God seems to shout. I pray for a difficulty to disappear, and the problem fades. I tell everyone that God answers prayers because what I wanted to change has been changed.

I pray for someone who is sick to be well, and she improves. Next Wednesday night at the church's prayer meeting, I tell everyone that God hears and God responds. God did what I asked.

I take a test. I'm sort of prepared, but I could have used a few more hours to read more about Amos and Hosea.

However, the question is about the prophet, Jeremiah. Would you believe that is exactly what I studied? After the test, I tell my friends that God answers prayer. Of course, if the question had dealt with Amos, then God would have been silent, and my conviction about the active God who listens to my pleadings would have been greatly diminished.

Whether we believe God is active in our lives depends on the way in which we perceive God works. To say God works in ways that I want is to reverse the creation saga and to create God in my image. Granted, what we ask for is what we believe is best and is born from caring motives. God does ask us to bring our concerns to the Holy One. We can quote Scriptures that indicate that if we are sincere and faithful, God does listen to the cries of the Creator's children.

Yet, other passages of Scripture remind us that God is God and that our ways and our wills are not always God's way and God's will. Experientially, we are reminded every day that bad things happen to good people and good things happen to those who have little or no interest in things of the Spirit.

Praying to the God of Mystery

Every Wednesday night when I gather with a community of believers to share in a prayer meeting, I'm reminded that what we do is no simple equation. We all may wish that our faith plus God's love always brings healing, restoration, or renewal in the church we love. However, we've prayed enough to know that someone for whom we prayed so fervently died last week from cancer. John lost his job; Dave and Maxine are still getting a divorce; Audrey goes home to an alcoholic husband who, despite our fervent intercession, still has no use for the One whom we profess brings meaning to our lives.

While those of us who preach may still speak passionately about a God who loves and hears us, we need to be careful that we are not accessories to people's disillusionment. Not only is it unbiblical, but also it is dishonest to preach about a God who always gives us what we believe is best. When we believe in this God who continually "fails" us, we eventually stop talking to God because God seems to have stopped talking to us.

Among other lessons, David's illness has reminded me that I always see through the glass darkly. When I pray, I speak to a God who is still a mystery to me. I can't explain. I can't understand. Most of all, I can't make it all right or at least what seems all right to me. In fact, I can't even say God has some great plan, and, therefore, I accept pain and suffering as a part of some divine scheme God has for David or for us.

I can lament. I can be angry with God. I can ask God to use the lingering grief to help tenderize me and to remind me that ultimately I'm not in control of so many things in my life or in the lives of others. I can pray for the strength to make it through the day and to respond graciously to the anticipated and the unanticipated.

I sat with a group of ministers at an ordination council for a young couple. Both Stephanie and Brandon are talented, bright, compassionate, and committed to being

Christian ministers. One of the pastors around the table has a fifteen-year-old son with muscular dystrophy. Some of us were trying to tell Brandon and Stephanie that as ministers, we continue to try to offer our care to others even when things around us aren't what we may like. The pastor whose child was ill told a story. It was so much more powerful than any of the other words some of us had spoken.

"This morning," Jeff said, "I awoke at 5:00 as I do every day to give my son a bed bath, get him dressed, and fix his breakfast. This morning was especially difficult because my son hadn't slept well. After struggling to get him bathed," Jeff said, "I turned my son over and when I did, his hand brushed mine. When his hand touched mine, he kept it there as if to say, 'In spite of everything, I love you, Dad, and am grateful for your care for me.'" With tears in his eyes, Jeff spoke what all of us ministers know. There are times in our lives when we wonder where God is, when the difficulties of our ministry seem too much, and, perhaps, the touch of a child's hand becomes God's whisper to the most moving matters of life and an example of the strength God gives us to make it through whatever we face.

Would David have made his father proud if he had finished medical school or law school? Would he have made me proud if he told me he wanted to be a minister like his dad? Of course! Any of those things would have made me proud. I could easily have said, "God has heard my prayers and given me a child who will make a difference." I could shout, "God has answered by prayers and given me what I wanted!"

That's not our story. However, I can't help believing that God has given us a better gift. We have a son who touches

WHEN GOD APPEARS TO GROW SILENT

our hands and, most of all, touches our lives. David tells Diane and me that he loves us and is thankful that we are a family.

David, you have blessed us in ways too deep for words, and when your dad takes time to be still and silent, I know how much God has spoken to me through your life. David, I love you.

Chapter Five

Listening for the Still, Small Voice

Imagining God

How do you and I imagine God? I realize that God exceeds our capacities for imagination, but most of us live with some mental image of the Divine. It's almost necessary. For example, when I pray, I can't speak with any intimacy to something that is formless, shapeless, and total mystery.

When Jesus spoke about the One who had sent him, he said, "Father." Is that image exhaustive of all that God is? Of course not! Does the metaphor have limitations? Ask someone whose earthly father has abused him, and a lot of pain has to be unpacked before the term "father" can be redeemed.

Yet, we continue to use mental images of the Holy One because we need ways to connect with the God we love but don't see. As a child I always envisioned God as male, old, kind, and sitting down. God smiled a lot, was overweight, and in many ways looked like the Santa Claus who appeared at the department store during Christmas. I knew God was responsible for a log of big stuff, but I figured God had done most of that before reaching this doddering stage of life.

If God became angry, God didn't remain that way, although I recognized the things I did that would raise God's ire at least until I had asked God's forgiveness. Things like drinking, cussing, talking back to my parents, and dancing with the opposite sex. I suppose God may have been angry if I danced with members of the same sex, but at the time that wasn't a pressing issue. At the junior high dances, girls danced with girls because they finally gave up on the boys walking across the gym floor to ask one of them to "fast dance." The issue was dancing because it led to "other things," which at the time I wouldn't have even considered if the preacher had not brought up those "other things."

Regardless, God seemed kind but relatively passive. Of course, the more I learned about the God of the Bible, the more I changed my image of God. God was involved. God was active. God was seeking to draw us back to God's love and grace.

Yet, God always seemed to give us a choice about our response. God invited, but God didn't impose. God called, but God didn't coerce. As a minister, I was called to be a voice to extend God's invitation. At times, my own desire to see things happen or my insecurity that people or things were not changing in ways that I wanted caused me to cross the line between invitation and imposition. After all, wouldn't it be so much easier on God and all of us if God shouted and never gave us the option of saying "no"?

However, that's not the way the grace of God seems to work. In the biblical witness, God shouts periodically, but

more often God speaks in the whispers of events, other per-
sons, or circumstances we encounter. Since God whispers,
that means those of us on the receiving end have to become
good listeners as well as interpreters of the messages we
believe are from God.

I often hear people say God told them to do this or God
led them in some unmistakable way in their lives. For me,
the voice of God has been more nuanced. Frankly, I've
envied those to whom the Divine One speaks through the
fire or the strong wind. I have felt gentle breezes, but I didn't
know for sure where the breeze had begun or where it was
trying to take me in my life.

To say God speaks in a still, small voice and that we have
to interpret that voice raises several implications. I live with
the humility that I may misjudge or misinterpret, but that
God can work through the mistakes of my life. In a profound way, this removes the burden from me of always
trying to interpret God correctly. For example, many people
speak of God's having a perfect plan for our lives and insist
that our responsibility is to discern and follow that plan.

While I don't deny that God has plans and desires for
each of us, I have difficulty in saying that I see those plans
clearly or am able to follow them correctly. But if God
moves us through life like a master chess player, what does
that do to our free will? What does that do to the grace of
God that permits us to say no as well as yes? What does that
do to divine Love that issues invitations instead of sending
us on forced marches?

I look around my office at the numerous pictures of my
grandson. In one picture, I'm holding Finn, and I'm reading

a book to him. He was about four months old, and he let his Grampa set our direction. Now Finn is almost four years old. When Finn came to visit recently, he wanted no part of Grampa's reading to him. He wants to read himself.

He and I go into our "magic room," which is filled with his books and mine. Finn has a chair of his own, and he pulls it beside mine. He selects two books from his shelf. He reads one and gives me the other. What makes this interesting is that we read aloud at the same time. Then we trade books, and both of us read aloud again.

Finn doesn't get all the words right. In fact, some of what he says he's reading isn't found in the book at all. A picture of a dog may send Finn into an imaginative tale of a dog who is happy because he's being patted by a little boy.

What is happening between my grandson and me is about more than dogs, little boys, or even reading books. On the surface, the whole scene of our reading at the same time sounds chaotic. In a way it is. However, what I like is listening to my grandson's emerging voice, the voice of Finn whom I deeply love.

It's an unfinished voice. It's a child's voice, soft but warm and filled with wonder at a world becoming alive through books that take us on wonderful journeys. I like the velvet feel of his voice, and though Finn doesn't say all the words right, it's his voice that stops my reading once in a while so I can listen to the dog who is happy because the little boy patted him.

Sometimes I even think I hear something of God's voice in my grandson's words. Chalk it up to grandfatherly pride, but while Finn is saying nothing overtly religious, he is reminding me of deep things like love, simplicity, and wonder.

How different from the way most of the rest of life arrives at my ear and finally at my heart. It's shrill. Somebody is yelling at me on television to buy a car from his dealership. An attractive young woman tells me I need a new carpet, and in the television commercial she races from one rug to another shouting that I can't live without a new rug, and my wife and I need to come to the rug outlet store.

Even church can be loud. I hope it's just not my age, but I really don't like somebody's telling me that I need to give God applause or I have to clap my hands to make a joyful noise. My life is already filled with lots of noise, and, frankly, I believe I may lean forward if something profound is said in a whisper. I may even listen if the minister says, "Let's be still." No words—no background music; listening to the silence and through the silence, hoping that we may know that there is a God who is with us.

When I was in elementary school, I remember the so-called "Quaker Days" we had during lunchtime. Our school cafeteria was like most school cafeterias, with clattering of dishes and silverware, scraping of chairs on the floor, and all of us talking to and about each other. Once in a while, though, our teachers would declare a "Quaker Day." In fourth grade, I didn't know much about the Quakers except that the teacher told us they were people who knew how to be quiet and who actually enjoyed silence.

I didn't realize it at the time, but I'm sure that the teachers instituted the day so they could enjoy their lunches and have a reprieve from the noise. As students, we actually liked it. It was different. We walked softly into the cafeteria, quietly picked up our trays, gently placed our silverware on our napkins, and didn't talk. When we finished eating, we lifted our chairs away from the tables so we wouldn't make that grinding noise on the floors.

Years later, when I had the chance to worship in a Society of Friends' meeting, I recalled my "Quaker Days" at Fairlawn Elementary in Miami, Florida. As I worshipped with these folks who didn't seem compelled to fill the air with the steady stream of words, I was deeply moved. Silence wasn't a gap between sounds. It was a moment of "holy listening" when God spoke without anyone's having to speak for God.

Listening Before We Speak

As our family moved into the valley of David's suffering, I realized again how programmed I was to speak and sometimes to claim that as a minister I spoke God's words. Of course, the assumption made by those who listened to me was that before I spoke for God, I had listened to God. After all, I had been called to preach, been prepared for it through the right education, and, thus, the listeners had the right to certainty and assurance. The people who listened to me hardly wanted to know that I was preaching words that were only my words. The pulpit was the place for a word from God, and those words should be spoken cleanly, clearly, and crisply.

I have always had a love/hate relationship with preaching. I loved it because it was important. Words can make a difference in people's lives, and I relished the chance to try to make some difference for good. I liked preaching because I felt I had some gifts that matched my calling. By no means was I the consummate communicator in everyone's eyes, but I believed I had the capacity to articulate important things with energy and passion. As a young and middle-aged pastor, I moved to larger churches in our denomination, and those churches seemed to do well with me as their pastor. I preached, and most people seemed to think I had words from God.

Maybe I needed more "Quaker Days" in my life. I certainly needed to have more time and to take more time to focus on something other than just collecting a new set of words to carry with me to the pulpit. David continues to help me understand that silence is a good thing because it reminds us of our limits and lets us listen to the whispers and instructions of God.

The story of the prophet Elijah in 1 Kings 19 tells us that God is barely audible at times. Fleeing for his life, Elijah goes to the mountain of Horeb and spends the night in a cave. God calls the prophet from the cave and tells Elijah that the presence of God will be revealed. How God comes is the surprise of the story. The loud noises come in a succession of violent wind, earthquake, and fire. But each time, we are told that God is not in any of those. Finally, the gentle whisper of God comes, and in that still, small voice, the Divine begins to restore the courage of the prophet. Elijah returns to the place of his greatest fear.

The Silence with Which We Live

When you and I face something overwhelming, we look for the courage to face what makes us afraid. When David was first diagnosed with his tumor, he and all of our family experienced a lot of noise. There were the noises of hospitals, the sounds of friends who came to support us, and the phone calls from people who let us know of their concerns and prayers.

This is usually the response to the grief of someone for whom we care. We want to let that person know we sympathize. We embrace those who are grieving, and even if we don't know what to say, our expressions of care speak loudly to those we love.

However, the fact is that none of us can maintain the intensity of our initial response. We have our own lives and other people for whom we care. We have demands on our time and attention. None of us intentionally forgets about people who are hurting, but our lives become full, and we assume that the passage of time is helping to bind the wounds of those who are hurting.

It's been more than twenty-four years since our son became ill, and most of the noise has ceased. Certainly, people still care. Friends still ask about David, but we all understand that responses can't be maintained at the same intensity. Now, our family listens with the gift of some time to adjust to this new reality. We try to listen to whispers and to the silence.

God's coming to Elijah in the still, small voice or gentle whisper is more remarkable when you look at the story of

Elijah. He was a prophet in public. Elijah's battle with the 500 prophets of Baal was a public performance. The story has the "feel" of wind, earthquake, and fire. Surely, God should come to Elijah in expected ways, but the surprise is the soft sound of the Divine.

As a minister, I've never had a day like Elijah. I've never had any moment when I seemed to conquer evil with anything like Elijah's success. However, I have come to love the public moments, perhaps more than I should, and to enjoy the sounds of affirmation, again more than I should.

I see my son sitting across the room looking at a magazine. Nobody says anything, but I think about how grateful I am to have him. David has been and is my teacher. Not a teacher in the sense of someone formally instructing me, but David is a teacher if I pay careful attention.

For example, several nights ago I came home after preaching at a church. It was about 10:00 at night. I was tired because I had been preaching for five nights and making the drive to the church in another town. The days had been cluttered with the expected and unexpected concerns a dean faces at the job. I noticed driving home that I was feeling a sense of "letdown." While I complain about busyness, I know the noise, the excitement, and the interactions feed the part of me that needs to be needed.

When I parked the car in the driveway, I stepped out of the car, and there was David to meet me. He helped me carry my briefcase and coat into the house. As we walked together to the front door, David said, "Dad, how are you?" He said the words softly, almost in a whisper.

"I'm fine, David," I said, "and I feel even better after seeing you." You will understand when I say that David will never speak like the wind, the earthquake, or the fire. That's not his nature. David is the gentle whisper.

That is exactly what I needed. Much of my life is lived in relationships with people where I am their preacher, their dean, or their colleague. Most people never ask how I'm doing, and to be honest, I don't ask enough people how they're doing. We are interested in furthering agendas, getting a project accomplished, fashioning a vision, or preaching a sermon that at least makes people think we have some semblance of idea about what we're doing.

With David, there is no agenda other than the agenda of a son's caring for his father. Maybe when you've faced death squarely in the face, you get a better sense of what matters in life. So what if Elijah defeats the prophets of Baal? So what if he is on top of his world one day but then collapses under the weight of Jezebel's threat the next day? For all of us, it is a reminder of the ebb and flow of our lives. Our agenda is to succeed, but what do we do when we fail?

In fall 2004, I had the opportunity to audit a class taught by Dr. Ronald Heifetz. Heifetz teaches at the John F. Kennedy School of Government at Harvard University. The leadership class I took was an introduction to Heifetz's understanding of "adaptive leadership."

Most of the students in the class were working on a Master's degree. Many of them already had experience as government leaders, business executives, and a host of other exciting ventures. They were attending Harvard not because they had failed miserably in life but because they were bright, energetic, and the places where they served wanted them to develop all of their potential.

On the second day of class, Heifetz divided us into groups and told us that he wanted each of us to write a case study on some failure in our leadership. The reaction of many in the class was swift and furious. To acknowledge a failure, much less to write about it so other people were aware of it, was out of the question. One student expressed it well when she said, "It didn't work out the way I envisioned, but given the circumstances and people with whom I was working, nobody could have done a better job than I did."

I may not have said it that bluntly, but I engage in the same kind of "scapegoating" in my own life. As a minister, as an educator, as a husband, as a father, as anything, I look for the failing outside myself. Sometimes the fault is elsewhere, but sometimes it is with me or at least I'm an accessory to the failure.

Like Elijah, I like to think of myself as a bold person with bold vision and bold words. The fact is that I am not so many times. Something or someone makes me afraid, and I would like to find the nearest cave.

"Dad, how are you?" David says as he and I walk the few steps to the house. David is asking about me. Whether I did a good job is not the issue. Whether the people who heard me thought that I was a good preacher, a fair preacher, or they couldn't wait for the benediction isn't the issue. When you have come to the brink of death, I suppose it puts life into perspective. I succeed and I fail. Some people like me. Others don't, and a whole lot of folks have better things to

do than sitting around trying to decide whether they like me
or not.

God speaks in the whisper of grace in the soft voice of a
child who loves me because I'm his dad. David also reminds
me of the joys that come from what many of us would label
"minor accomplishments." As many of us get older, we realize we are not going to achieve all we set out to do in our
lives. Equally important, we recognize that we are not going
to be all we thought we might be. People like Albert
Schweitzer and Mother Teresa, selfless and gifted people,
once served as our role models. With the passing of years, we
recognize that we are not like them, and it brings us a certain sadness.

Ways of doing and being that we saw as goals are now
considered out of reach. We see the distance between our
aspirations and our accomplishments. We understand that
the people who have lived with us and know us best recognize that we are a strange mix of self-centeredness and
selflessness. At best, this recognition gives us humility to
understand that God uses us, but God does not depend on
us.

When our grandson and daughter came to visit us, I
watched a beautiful moment unfold. David is embarrassed
when we praise him or draw attention to something he's
done. On this day, however, I could see the joy in David's
eyes. Finn and David were on a swing set. Finn wanted to
swing like his Uncle Dave. But Finn couldn't get the right
motion of his legs to go up and back.

I watched David slow down and then gently show Finn
how to move his legs. Finn never really got the timing. His

legs would go out too late or come back too quickly, but David was so patient. I could see the look of joy on my son's and grandson's faces as Finn looked to his Uncle Dave for guidance.

I realize that teaching a child to swing won't make the newspaper. It happens every day, but which of us can't remember the time that we learned to swing and the person who helped us? To other people it may seem ordinary, but we remember it as a "rite of passage."

As I watched David, I thought again about how God speaks softly through the tender moments of life. As a minister, much of my life is spent trying to do something, say something, or be something to others. Because much of what I do is public, I'm evaluated sometimes formally and many times informally.

More than I would like to admit, I'm concerned about outcomes and what people think of me. I lose the tenderness, the kindness, or the simplicity that once gave birth to who I am or what I do. I'm too "other-directed." What do people think of me, and how am I doing? The joy is lost.

Then I watch two swings on a swing set late in the afternoon. I see my child finding great joy in helping his nephew. Who says God doesn't speak in a quiet way? David teaches his dad that joy isn't always or even often found in the wind, the earthquake, or the fire. Simple things, soft words—God passes our way, and we ponder the unexpected ways that God works.

Chapter Six

Living One Moment at a Time

Questions That Have No Answers

Shortly after David was diagnosed with his tumor, Diane and I sat down with the neurosurgeon to talk about David's prognosis and treatments. I wanted to know what we could expect. Would David get well? Would he be the same David we had known before his illness?

I expected the doctor to have the answers. After all, he was the expert. He had studied these things. He had attended medical school so that he could give assurance to families like ours who were facing uncertain futures.

I had always perceived physicians to be better than ministers at providing answers. In fact, I have been envious of doctors who walked into a patient's room with a protocol for treatment, while as a minister, I would walk in to tell people that I couldn't explain their suffering, but that I would walk with them through the uncertainty.

It's hard to chart a minister's kind of care. What do I write down? I have no prescription pad. I represent God in some sense, but does that ever give me the right to tell someone, "I know that this is the way God is working"? What I did as a minister seemed so tentative compared to the physician who said, "Take this pill or follow this protocol, and you will feel better."

That's why I was so surprised when I asked the doctor about my son's prognosis. With as much tentativeness as I had felt as a minister, our neurosurgeon replied, "We'll do what we can, and then we will take things one day at a time."

How profoundly disappointed I was at his response. I expected that he would tell me the precise nature of David's illness, the treatment he prescribed, and what he was going to do the fix our problem.

Problem/Solution

In his book *Preaching*, Fred Craddock says that a popular design preachers use for sermons is "Problem-Solution." In twenty-five minutes or so, the minister stands in front of her congregation and says, "Here's the problem; here's the solution!" It's a "clean" way to preach. You don't have to mess with ambiguities. You don't confuse the congregation with, "It may be this or it may be that or it may be none of these." The minister is the oracle bringing the clear word of God to every confusing situation.

Of course, Craddock suggests that this is one form for a sermon, and there's good reason that it's not the one and only form. Frankly, little of life is lived with that king of clarity. The world in which we live is complex, and our own lives are complex. For example, when a person is depressed, a multitude of systems are interlaced. There may be a spiri-

tual component, but there is also the biological, the neuro-
logical, the emotional history of the person, and other
factors that feed the depression. To suggest that depression is
a spiritual problem easily solved by trusting God more is a
vast oversimplification that only complicates the spiritual
inadequacy many of us feel.

In fact, the more we understand systems' theory, the
more complex and interrelated we understand things to be.
Our bodies are systems. When one part of our body has a
problem, our whole body focuses its attention on the part
that is hurting.

When I was about fourteen, I was playing baseball. The
batter on the other team got a hit to left field. A runner was
on second base. He was trying to score on the hit. I was
playing shortstop. Our left fielder picked up the ball and
threw it to me. My job was to catch the ball, throw it to our
catcher, and tag the other team's runner before he scored. In
my eagerness to catch and throw in one fluid motion, I put
my right hand in front of my glove, and the relay throw
broke my index finger. Don't ask if we won the game.
Frankly, I don't care. My finger hurt so badly that night that
the rest of my body sat up with my finger.

All Is Connected

At the time, I had no idea what systems' theory was.
However, I knew that if one part of my body were hurting,
all of me would be hurting. What's true of our physical
bodies is true of families, organizations, or any type of com-

munity, church, or group. When something goes wrong in a connected group, the entire community feels the ripples.

Since David's illness, I have come to appreciate the inter-relatedness of most things and the subsequent complexity. While I wanted a clear, concise diagnosis with an equally clear protocol of treatment and prognosis, the fact was that David's illness was far more complex. Apparently, the tumor had originated on the pineal gland of his brain. The physician had no idea what had precipitated the cancer. "Perhaps," he said, "this was a congenital defect that took ten years to grow to the point where it exhibited symptoms."

What David's physicians did determine was that the malignancy had metastasized and was now present in his pituitary gland. Perhaps the tumor had also invaded the central nervous system—thus the need later to radiate both David's head and central nervous system. Cancer had invaded one part of our son's body, but it was affecting all of David's body. If left untreated, the disease would eventually result in the death of David's whole physical system. We were not dealing with a clear "problem-solution" formula.

At times, the doctors would give Diane and me options about David's treatment, and I recall how angry I was that our family was being asked to make decisions about problems that far exceeded our expertise. They were the doctors. They had been to medical school. Our insurance company was paying them sizeable chucks of money for their knowledge and expertise. Yet, the surgeon said, "Here are the options. What do you want to do?"

Not long ago I went to see an endodontist about a root canal. He knew I was a minister. After my mouth was

numbed and he was drilling my tooth, he started telling me
about a theology class he was taking at his home church. He
was excited about what he was learning, but I could tell
quickly that he and I had some significant differences in our
theology.

"What do you think about creationism?" my dentist
asked. Of course, I couldn't answer because he had his drill
in my mouth. So he did what a lot of dentists do. He gave
answers to his own questions. "My pastor showed us how
dinosaurs could have existed, and the world could still have
been created in 4004 BC." At that point, I was glad I could-
n't answer because he had the drill and I had a numbed
mouth with saliva coming out of both sides of a mouth I
could barely feel.

As I sat in his chair, my dentist regaled me with some
other theological tidbits that his pastor assured him were
true. He also told me that his minister had warned him
about theological liberals who didn't believe the Bible.

I have to give my endodontist credit. He did a wonderful job on my tooth. I don't doubt that he's an expert on
teeth. All of his diplomas were on the wall. As far as I could
tell, he is an educated endodontist. If he had talked to me
about root canals, he would have had my full attention. I
wouldn't have understood some of the technical language,
but I would have believed whatever he said about dentistry.

When he moved into theology, he lost me. Understand
that I don't comprehend a lot of things that fit under the
large tent of theology. I have learned to live with mystery
and to recognize that there are legitimate differences of opin-
ion. I even have some friends who believe Archbishop Usher

was precisely right when he calculated that God created the world in 4004. What I have trouble with is the idea that if we don't agree, then we are "liberals" who don't believe the Bible.

My dentist had moved outside the circle of his expertise. I suppose much of dentistry is precise. I'm guessing there's not much ambiguity in what a dentist does. The dentist may say, "I'm going to try to keep this tooth, but we may not be able to save it." However, I've never had a dentist say, "Let's pray about the decision to see what God wants us to do." I love God, but at that point, I'm more concerned about what the dentist believes is the wiser choice.

Yet, the physicians who treated David gave us choices. While I felt inadequate to deal with these decisions, I suppose it was the doctor's way of saying they could offer no guarantees on any procedure. Since David was our son, Diane and I needed to decide because any of the decisions we might make would have ramifications for the way David's body would function. For example, one surgery David had involved the remote possibility that David would be left sightless. No part of his body existed in isolation. Our son was a system as well as our child, and who knew what might be affected.

Stress on the Family

Similarly, we discovered our family was a system. David's diagnosis meant our whole family system was tilted. Our thirteen-year-old daughter was adjusting to a recent family move, a new school, and all the other changes that come with being a teenager. Suddenly, we weren't able to give her the emotional focus and support she needed.

My wife and I also knew about the marriages of friends that hadn't survived the serious illness or death of a child. Attention and care we had shared with each other were suddenly devoted to a son who needed our love as he had never needed it before. Of course, the biggest problem was that we were all emotionally depleted and having to draw on personal resources that seemed so limited.

A friend of mine compared this experience to our having a bank account. We make withdrawals but have little to deposit. Finally, one day we write a check only to discover that there is nothing left in the account. In effect, I kept making emotional withdrawals but hardly had time to think about keeping myself spiritually and emotionally solvent. My focus was David. That meant I had little time to listen to others whom I loved or to care for them. Our family system was broken, and we were all adjusting to the needs of our son.

Those who deal with an ongoing grief situation in their lives have to begin by recognizing that their family system has been disrupted, and the question becomes, "How do we respond?" Obviously, the brokenness of a child who is sick can surface a number of unresolved issues in a family.

One spouse blames the other for what's happened. None of us can think clearly in moments of overwhelming sadness, and we struggle to find an answer to why this happened. A part of this response may be blaming. I sat one day during the midst of David's most difficult days and thought about whether our son's tumor was a result of cancer on my side of the family or on Diane's side. Thinking about that now makes me embarrassed and even ashamed. I suppose it was part of a desperate search to determine why David's tumor was malignant. In moments of desperation, we scramble for answers to try to make sense of what seems so senseless. I thought that if I could find the answer or, more particularly, pin the blame on someone other than myself, it would give me some resolution.

I'm grateful that Diane's and my marriage was strong enough to bear the strain of trying to care for our son and to deal with the resulting anger and sadness. As in so many instances, my anger became displaced. I didn't feel that I could become angry with David, and the tumor was so impersonal; I didn't know how to be angry with a tumor.

Feeling Distant from God

With God, I did become angry. Ironically, at the time I most needed to feel the closeness of this God in whose name I preached each Sunday, I felt so distant. I didn't stop believing in God as much as I wondered, "Where is God in all of this?" As a pastor, I must often deal with the pain of others. While I never tried to gloss over the hurt of others by saying God cares, God understands, and God knows pain first-hand, that was the underlying theological premise out of which I offered pastoral care.

"Yea, though I walk through the valley of the shadow of death," the psalmist wrote, "I will fear no evil, for thou art

with me." In Matthew's Gospel, Joseph, in the middle of all
the uncertainly that God had brought into his and Mary's
lives, was called to remember the words of Isaiah. God has
always been with us a "suffering servant," and this new revelation of God will be called "Emmanuel," which means
"God with us."

As a disciple and as a proclaimer of the good news, I had
to believe more than just "God is." The mere existence of a
God was not sufficient. Who is that God? How does that
God relate to humankind? Is our fundamental identity
simply creations from whom God keeps great distance? Or
are we children for whom God feels deep love?

The issue for me hasn't been so much whether "God is."
Rather, I wonder, "Is this God with us?" Is Emmanuel
simply a name or is it a fundamental reality? On a human
level, we have all heard of or perhaps even experienced the
sadness of a child who was physically abused by the man she
called "Daddy." All children have a right to expect that their
parents will be with them in caring and constructive ways.
How devastating it must be to trust someone as a child
trusts a parent, and then to have that trust abused so vio-
lently.

This was a theological and personal issue. Not only did I
believe in God, but also I trusted God. What was happening
to David and to our family felt like abuse. Perhaps God
didn't cause this directly, but God allowed it to happen. In
theory, we can differentiate between God's permissive will
and God's direct will. We can talk about the consequences of
humanity's disobedience and how the ripples of that sin
wash onto the shores of those who seem most innocent.

But when the pain becomes personal, explanations like this become less satisfying. How do we look at the face of a son whose hair has fallen out from radiation treatments and whose face is bloated from steroids and say, "God, the good God, the God who is with us, has permitted this to happen to you"? "What have I done, Dad, to deserve this?" "Nothing, my child, but this is a fallen world, and bad things happen to good people."

I had a faculty colleague whose adult son suffered from schizophrenia. Like many people suffering from this mental illness, the son would go off and on his medications. The side effects of the medications were difficult, and when he felt better, he thought he no longer needed them. This created a spiral in which the delusional thinking reappeared, and the symptoms of the illness reasserted themselves.

My colleague and his wife often wondered not only about how their son was doing but also where he was living. Did he have a place to sleep? Did he have something to eat? Periodically, their child would check himself into a mental health facility for treatment, but once he felt better, he was back on the streets.

What do I say to those two people who are the epitome of compassion and care? "This is a fallen world, and whether you've been good or not, your teeth have been set on edge. You are a victim of a crime that you didn't commit, unless we say that because we are a part of the human family, we are all as guilty as sin."

Living Our Theology

The problem is that our theology does not offer us much comfort precisely at the moment when we need comfort. I found no solace in the fact that it rains on the just and the unjust. Making distinctions between God's direct will and permissive will didn't help me to accept what had happened.

That's why I suggest that we live one moment at a time. First, it really is the way the Bible suggests that we live. One of the most incredible things about Jesus' call to discipleship is the way he invited people to breathe deeply the air of the moment in which they were living. Feeling remorseful about the past simply froze them in a time that was no longer theirs to live. Forgiveness was the attitude. Regret keeps us bound to feeling sorry about what has been written in the stories of our lives.

At the same time, anxiety about the future makes little sense. As my mentor John Claypool said, "We are living in a time not our own." We all make plans, but when the plans preempt the experience of the present, we move into a time that is really not ours. Besides, chronic anxiety does nothing constructive to help us face whatever future God gives us.

We have this moment—pleasant, painful, expected, and unexpected. We learn from our successes and our failures. If we are open, we may learn that life is lived dependent upon God. This is far different from trying to explain how God works. Rather, it recognizes the mystery that is at the heart of life and that the mystery brings us the range of experiences and emotions. Can I trust God with my fears, my doubts, and my sadness that life has not worked the way I expected? Can I live without understanding everything or explaining everything? Can I trust God in the moment even when my mind asks, "Where is this 'Emmanuel,' and how is God with me?"

Not long ago, one of my African American students preached a stirring sermon about living the moment we are given. With beautiful eloquence, he spoke about how it will be all right "in a little while." Rhetorically, he asked, "When is a little while?" "We don't know," he replied. "We just know that God will work it out in God's little while."

Much of black preaching is planted in the rich soil of trust in God's providential care. Born out of oppressive times when there was little control of their lives, the slaves lived in this moment because it was all they had, and they trusted God with their lives. These oppressed people had no control over their futures, but they believed God was giving them strength to live the moment.

The Bible doesn't predict the future. Rather, in apocalyptic documents like Revelation, God is in our present and is working God's purpose for the not yet. "Tears will be wiped away," but in this moment our tears teach us that pain is a part of our lives. If we don't become jaded, we may learn that each of us is built to depend on God.

This moment is all we have. Living in the moment may also help us realize that to postpone the kind words we want to speak or the good things we want to do is to risk running out of time. When David was diagnosed, I thought often about the priorities of my life. I could be the "poster child" for the affliction that how we imagine ourselves is related to what we achieve. As far back as I can remember, this has been a part of "DNA."

My family laughs about an experience I share with them from my kindergarten days. The teacher was telling us how to make music with sticks we hit together and little triangles that we rang. After we had banged the sticks and hit the triangles for a while, the teacher said our class was going to be a part of a program at the Bayfront Park Bandshell in downtown Miami, Florida. The program would be at night so that all of our parents could attend.

Our teacher told us we would be playing "Old MacDonald Had a Farm." "Does anyone know the song? We need a leader," she said. I had never heard the song, but the possibility to lead and to be out front overwhelmed my integrity. "I know the song," I shouted, and so I was chosen to lead the band.

Fortunately, none of the members of the class knew much, if any, music, so the night of the performance, I stood in front vigorously waving my arms as the band played in the way that they would have played with or without me. My recollection is that if someone listened carefully, once in a while you could hear something that sounded like a note from "Old MacDonald."

Where Do We Live?

Living in the future or living in the past are options for all of us, especially when the present is painful. Turning back the calendar to a time when all our family had to deal with were the ordinary frustrations and challenges of life was a way to escape the pressures of the present. For a brief moment, I could go back to the goodness of the garden. But the serpent does its work, and we realize that returning to Eden is an illusion. We have left the garden, and life is as life is. That means life happens to us and in us, and often our only choice is how we respond.

Living in the future is another option. When my children were small, they would sometimes close their eyes to avoid looking at something unpleasant. One day my son fell off his bicycle and cut his knee. We took David to the hospital for stitches.

Laura Beth went with us to the hospital, and she had her eyes closed the whole trip. "Does it make you feel badly to see your brother bleed?" Diane asked. "It makes me feel bad," Laura Beth answered, "but it also makes David's hurt go away when I don't have to look at it."

Not a bad idea if you can do it! Just close your eyes to the pain, and maybe it won't be there when you look again. The only problem with this approach is that it doesn't work. Difficulties exist whether I want to see them or not. I can go to bed, pull up the covers, close my eyes, and try to escape. It's called avoidance. Some people develop avoidance into an art form. We avoid by pretending the issue is not there, by blaming someone else, by not showing up, and in countless other ways.

Most of us don't like conflict or difficulties. We spend our time hoping the problem will go away by itself or that someone else will solve it for us. Maybe, by not doing anything or closing our eyes, the bleeding will stop. So we choose to say or do nothing, but the bleeding continues.

To live in the moment is to say the words of gratitude, to give the love we feel for others, or to encourage the friend who is struggling. But it's also to open our eyes to the bleeding in ourselves, to those around us, and to a world where there is a lot of bleeding. This isn't pleasant. However, it is a part of reality that demands the courage of our seeing it before we can begin to live into it. Accepting what is rather than wishing for something that doesn't exist won't always make us happy, but it opens us to what we may learn in the moment.

I think about people I have known who have been married to spouses with dementia. How sad it must be to watch a life's partner sink into the fog of forgetfulness. We look through the scrapbook at pictures of vacations at the beach, children's birthday parties, or the moment we held our first grandchild. In the pictures, everyone is smiling, present to the experience of the moment. Now, we look across the room at the blank stare in our spouse's eyes and realize that the moments of being present are memories reflected in the yellow-edged pictures in the scrapbook.

How sad! Yet, I have seen a depth of love expressed by those who give care. The love is not reciprocated. Her beloved may not even recall her name. But she loves him with an unconditional love that is closer to what God's love must be like than almost any other expression of care. She remembers the words of the minister, the words she repeated to the young, handsome man standing next to her at the front of the church: "I, Martha, take you, Jim, to be my law-

fully wedded husband, for better or for worse, in sickness
and in health . . . ."

She had no idea what she was saying that day and all
that it implied. "For better or for worse," we say to each
other, but who of us in the full blossom of youth ever thinks
about the "worse"?

For Martha, it was now the "worse." The man she loved
had no capacity to love her. Yet, she kept loving Jim because
real love never ceases. Living in the moment—it may be
excruciatingly painful, but for those who behold it, it is
breathtaking in its beauty.

The God of the Now

Finally, we live in the moment because God is the God of
the now. I'm writing some of this during the Christian
season of Advent. I grew up in a Baptist church that did a
wonderful job of accenting one dimension of Advent.
Through Christmas pageants, cantatas, and through the
proclaimed Word, we moved into the first century and
adored the child who was the Christ. Most of our pageants
made no distinction between Matthew's account of the birth
and the story shared by Luke. Magi from the east stood by
children in bathrobes portraying the shepherds.

The whole time I was in the youth department, Claire
Lambert portrayed Mary. She was sweet, attractive, and per-
sonified what we thought about the mother of Jesus. Claire
was soft-spoken, and we could imagine her "pondering
something in her heart." The remainder of the cast changed,

but even the Christmas when Claire had braces on her teeth, we could accept it because we felt the mother of Jesus had perfect teeth.

So during Advent, our church remembered. We remembered a lot about the moment God came to earth. I wouldn't trade this experience for anything. It cemented in my mind that there was "earthliness" in this eternal God, and that God chooses to work in particular places with particular people at particular times.

What we didn't emphasize much during the Advent was the power of the present and even the anticipation of the future. Sermons about the second coming of Jesus were shared by attractive, articulate evangelists who managed to scare the daylights out of us. The second coming wasn't a hopeful promise of fulfillment. Rather, after hearing the sermon, most of us wondered if we would make it to the parking lot before God blew up the whole thing. If we made it to the parking lot, then we worried whether God would come just at the time we were doing or saying something we shouldn't.

The second coming, though, was not really a part of our Advent season. (By the way, we didn't use the word "Advent." We had Christmas and the days leading up to it.) Neither was the present emphasized. We believed God had done something significant in history. However, we never made the connection between that ancient manger and having mangers in our own hearts. Like most Baptist ministers, our pastor issued an invitation to be "saved," but I never saw any connection with the past, present, and future of life.

Jesus begins his public ministry in Luke's Gospel by announcing to the synagogue crowd in Nazareth, "Today this prophecy has been fulfilled in your hearing." To the original hearers, Jesus' words were jarring. "Today," Jesus began. The hearers could feel the urgency, the immediacy, the demand in his exposition of Isaiah. God had broken into history, and the dawning of the new day meant the dawning of a radically inclusive love.

Today—that is the challenge for some of us; to learn to live in our times because we have learned to forgive a past where our dreams have been dashed. We accept and even learn from the painful situations that have affected us. We look to the future not with dread but because God is with us on the journey. We live with expectancy because history itself and our whole personal histories are moving toward the moment when the Christ will be all and in all. We live toward a future, not because the end of this life fills us with dread and fear that God will catch us doing something wrong. Rather, in that final moment of these days and nights, all will be made right and the crooked ways will be made straight.

In the meantime, we have this moment. It is a gift from God. It may be a pleasant moment, and in that time we are filled with joy, and our gratitude comes easily. But our lives will have pain. Life isn't what we wished. Yet, we stay on our feet and keep walking. We keep walking with God and toward God. Who knows what may happen? If we keep walking, we may find some land that is "fairer than day." We may say, "The walk wasn't easy, but I'm grateful I had the privilege to walk and to know a son who continues to teach me so much."

Conclusion

You can probably tell from reading this book that the act of listening is not easy for me. I've been trained to talk, or more specifically to preach. In my vocation, I'm expected to "have" a word. Hearing a word is important, but even when I don't "hear" a word, I'm expected to "have" a word for the congregation.

Recently, I conducted a funeral for an eighty-five-year-old man who had been a member of the church where I am interim pastor. I knew this man's family, but the only time I had visited with J.Y. was in the hospital a few days before he died.

At the hospital, I introduced myself, but it was quickly apparent that he had no idea who I was. J.Y. and I talked for a few minutes, and then we had a word of prayer. I knew virtually nothing about him.

The day before the funeral I met with four members of the family. "I want you to talk about your father and grandfather while I listen. I'm going to write some things, but mainly, I want to listen to your memories." Once in awhile, I asked a question, but for more than forty minutes the family talked about J.Y. while I listened.

Hearing this family share their important recollections was a moving experience for me. I saw a man whom I knew very little recreated before my eyes. Memories of J.Y. poured out, and I heard about a man who was faithful to Christ and to the church. I also saw a man who liked a good game of "rook" and bingo, but who didn't like to lose at either. He loved baseball, his wife, his children, grandchildren and great-grandchildren. If one of his family members wanted a popsicle, "Paw-Paw" bought then a box of popsicles. "He always spoiled me," one of his granddaughters said, "and we always loved him for it."

I left the meeting with the family without saying much at all. I had listened, though, and in the process had been moved and touched. Why don't I listen more?

As you've read something of the story of my son David, you probably picked up quickly that I ran out of words to try to explain and understand what was happening. I was forced to be still and to listen, not a comfortable posture for me.

I wish I could tell you I have developed the art of listening. I would like to believe I have learned to keep my mouth shut and my ears open to "intimations of immortality."

If I told you that, it would not be true. However, I am trying to listen more to the pain and pleasures of life. I'm trying to be still more and listen to what God is teaching me.

David has helped me so much. The doctors say David depends on his dad. That may be true, but I depend as much on David.

David, I love you with all my heart.